RICHARD ANTHON

CH00408446

ROMANO-BRITISH COIN HOARDS

A hoard comes to light. The discovery of the Welbourn *nummus* hoard in a coarse-ware pot. As is typical, the top of the pot has long since been sheared off by ploughing, scattering the upper portion of the coins. The rest lie *in situ*, encircled by the broken edge of the sides of their container. (Photograph courtesy of finder, D. A. Phillips)

SHIRE ARCHAEOLOGY

2

Cover illustration
The Stanchester hoard from Wiltshire. Three gold *solidi*, thirty-three silver *miliarenses*, 1166 silver *siliquae* and a bronze *nummus* in an 'Alice Holt' coarse-ware pot. Date of latest coin: 406.

British Library Cataloguing in Publication Data:
Abdy, Richard.
Romano-British coin hoards. – (Shire archaeology; 82)
1. Coins, Roman – Great Britain
I. Title
737.4'9361
ISBN 0 7478 0532 6

Published in 2002 by
SHIRE PUBLICATIONS LTD
Cromwell House, Church Street, Princes Risborough,
Buckinghamshire HP27 9AA, UK.
(Website: www.shirebooks.co.uk)

Series Editor: James Dyer.

Copyright © Richard Anthony Abdy, 2002.

Richard Anthony Abdy is hereby identified as the author of this work in accordance with Section 77 of the Copyright, Designs and Patents Act, 1988.

All rights reserved.
No part of this publication may be reproduced or transmitted in any form or by any means, electronic or mechanical, including photocopy, recording, or any information storage and retrieval system, without permission in writing from the publishers.

Number 82 in the Shire Archaeology series.

ISBN 0 7478 0532 6.

First published 2002.

Printed in Great Britain by
CIT Printing Services Ltd, Press Buildings,
Merlins Bridge, Haverfordwest, Pembrokeshire SA61 1XF.

Contents

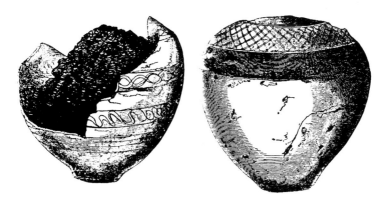

The two half-metre-wide storage jars that contained the Blackmoor hoard.
(Anonymous Victorian sketch)

4

List of illustrations

Note: All © The British Museum unless otherwise indicated in the caption. Unless indicated, individual coin images are reproduced at actual size.

Preface

This book is not really about hoards of 'Romano-British' coins (although short-lived Roman mints did operate in Britain, and local copying of Roman coins occurred throughout Roman times); it is about Roman coin hoards *found* in the former province(s) of Britannia. The character of these deposits is similar to those from other former Roman parts of north-west Europe, despite the later start and earlier end to Roman influence in Britain. Because of the size of the subject, only a minimum (and, I hope, representative) number of examples from each period has been used in order to highlight the general aspects of the subject.

An *Inventory of Romano-British Coin Hoards* – the life's work of its author, Anne Robertson – lists in 520 pages all hoards known up to 1992 (thereafter covered by volume X onwards of *Coin Hoards from Roman Britain*, edited by R. Bland *et al*). With this in mind, the present work will cover the bare essentials of Roman coin hoards from Britain and will focus where possible on examples that remain in the public domain to be visited. Indeed, many of the most spectacular and illuminating cases have been made in recent years and deserve more publication coverage. Finally, this work is intended to complement Shire's *Roman Coinage in Britain* by P. J. Casey, which provides an all-round introduction to the subject (monetary history, site coins and hoards) and was an early source of inspiration to the present writer.

I am very grateful for the help and advice of the following in producing this book: Donal Bateson, Roger Bland, Andrew Burnett, Stephen Dodd, Cathy King, Janet Larkin, Ian Leins, Tim Padley and Jonathan Williams.

Richard Anthony Abdy
Coins and Medals, The British Museum

Glossary

Early Roman Empire
This is the period from the first emperor (Augustus, 31 BC to AD 14) until, as far as Roman monetary history is concerned, the AD 260s. Its main coin denominations are:
As: copper – the smallest denomination applicable to Britain.
Aureus: gold – worth twenty-five *denarii*.
Denarius: silver – worth four *sestertii*.
Dupondius: brass – worth two *asses*.
Radiate: silver initially; becoming progressively baser – worth two *denarii*.
Sestertius: brass – worth two *dupondii*.

Later Roman Empire
Roughly the AD 270s onwards. Its main coin denominations were unstable and do not offer such a well defined relationship as before (and not all were produced at the same time). They are:
Miliarensis: large silver piece.
Nummus: silvered bronze until *c*.354, bronze thereafter.
Radiate: silvered bronze, i.e. containing such small amounts of silver that it remains base.
Siliqua: small silver piece.
Solidus: gold.

Other terms
Bronze: in numismatics, taken as a generic term for copper and copper-based alloys (including brass).
Closing date: the minting date of the latest coin in a hoard.
Coarse wares: rough pottery, usually local products, for everyday non-decorative functions and the commonest pottery containers for coin hoards. See Guy de la Bédoyère's *Pottery in Roman Britain* (Shire, 2000).
Debasement: the reduction in the intrinsic metallic value of a coin by reduction in size or dilution of its alloy with base metal.
Deposition date: the last time a hoard was seen by its erstwhile owner.
Gaul: the area now covered by France, and parts of the Rhineland and the Low Countries. (**Gallic** = of Gaul or the Gauls.)
Minting date: the date that a coin was made by being stamped or 'struck' with a design current at that point in time. The date of a coin is often expressed as the reign of an emperor, although archaeologists sometimes use 'coin periods' (see Casey, *Roman Coinage in Britain*, page 29).
RIC: *Roman Imperial Coinage*. The standard coin catalogue for the Empire in ten volumes. In volumes I–V, reference numbers are grouped under emperor; in VI–X, key references are volume/mint/number.
RRC: *Roman Republican Coinage*. The standard coin catalogue for the Republic by M. Crawford (Cambridge, 1974).

1
Roman coin hoards from Britain: an overview

Coin hoarding in Britain began when the Celtic people of the southern part of the island adopted coins in the second century BC and continued until at least the First World War. It reached a peak during the first four and a half centuries AD, from when a widespread and sophisticated Roman denominational system has left evidence of prolific hoarding of coins. The current number of recorded Roman hoards is approaching two thousand. It should always be remembered that the evidence is a residue of past activity, and hoards that survive today are only those that went unclaimed by their original owners.

Traditionally, historians have often sought to place the abandonment of hoards in the context of wider historical events such as warfare, and it is often the case that the number of unrecovered hoards increases during troubled times as disasters overtake their owners. This is seen, for example, with the large numbers of unrecovered coin hoards in both Italy during the Hannibalic war (218–201 BC) and Britain during the English Civil Wars (1642–8). The geographical distribution of the latter can be further linked not to the actual zones of conflict, but to the combatants' recruiting grounds. The problem is that such links are one step removed from the actual process and can only be made because historical sources survive; investigating the reasons for the abandonment of hoards from a largely ahistorical Roman Britain is a far more frustrating process. It is just as clear that, in the absence of banks, protecting savings by burial was simply common practice, and, with so many everyday reasons for abandonment, hoards rarely illuminate historical events any more than modern unclaimed bank accounts would illuminate today's history.

The nature of hoards

Other than studying where and how often hoards are found, it is also possible to use the contents of hoards as economic evidence of changes in the monetary system. As a collection of coins removed from circulation at the same time, a hoard should be a sample of the available coin population. A hoarder might make certain choices about what to hoard – for most of the Roman period silver coin was favoured because of its special importance in state payments and taxation. Unless there were particular reasons to avoid coins of certain periods (for example, debasement changes the relative intrinsic value of old and new coins), it is unlikely that a hoarder would bother to select older or newer coins in anything other than a random manner. Issues that had most presence in the general circulation should therefore have most presence in the hoard. The principle is similar to a handful of coins from a modern pocket. It would probably not contain many of the oldest possible types; these would as a group have faced the most attrition over time, becoming lost and replaced with new issues. Nor would it contain many of the most recent, since these are only just being released into circulation. Issues (replace this term with 'years' for modern coins and 'emperors' for Roman coins) that are most represented in a hoard should be somewhere in between the oldest and youngest coins present; when plotted on a graph they would form the crest of, typically, a skewed bell-curve, the earliest and latest coins being represented at the two tapering extremities nearest the *x*-axis.

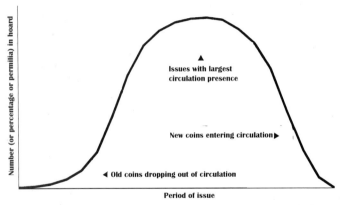

One implication of this pattern is the use of coins as dating tools in archaeology. If one coin had been dropped from the theoretical circulation represented by this curve, then the probability is that it would be one of the most numerous types. The most numerous types are represented by the crest of the curve; in contrast, both the most recent and the oldest coins available appear well away from this point – which implies that the newest coin would be about as likely to be dropped as the oldest! Date of minting is clearly one thing, but date of deposition is another, and a knowledge of how the coinage system developed and changed over time, for example by studying hoards, is indispensable in understanding finds of coins on archaeological sites. Recording the relationship of coins in their hoards has the same archaeological implications as, for example, considering artefacts in the context of grave groups. Romano-British hoards supply a series of partial snapshots of the coin circulation and indicate how long particular coins stayed in use (this could be hundreds of years), which types were supplied to Britain (not all Roman coins struck on the Continent were shipped to the island) and when certain coins were removed from general use.

Closing date

Identifying the date a hoard was abandoned is itself a problem. Abandonment must have occurred after the last coin it contains was minted – the 'closing date' of the hoard – but how near was it to the deposition date? In fact, the actual deposition date can never be known. However, statistically, the bigger the hoard, the more likely it is to contain an example of the latest possible coin to get into circulation and the more confident we can be that the closing and deposition dates are close. (The same is true of 'site' coins found in archaeological levels: the more coins there are from any particular context, the clearer the chronology.) By using closing dates, we can chart the recorded Roman coin hoards from Britain in a chronological distribution, and the resulting pattern can be seen in the graph below. (This is only a rough guide, since many older reports are unclear about the latest coin in the hoard.)

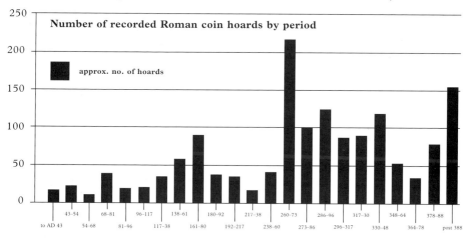

Types of coin hoards

A traditional classification has relied on looking at the presence of different issues in a hoard and judging the length of time it has been saved up. This would place hoards saved up over a lifetime in the category of 'savings' hoards, and those quickly put together in that of 'emergency' hoards. Studies of hoards from the second century (when Roman Britain was flourishing and the currency was stable and regularly supplied) have indicated that the time it took for coins of a certain emperor's reign, after being struck and delivered to Britain, to reach a maximum presence in the British circulation (the crest of the curve), before being withdrawn and hoarded, could be twenty to thirty years. In most cases, this is after the death of the emperor whose image was on the coin, a process too slow to show a meaningful difference over one saver's lifetime. The savings/emergency accumulation-time categorisation is therefore not clear-cut and most hoards lie at an indefinable point between the two extremes. Exceptions are 'purse' hoards, small packets of coins that would not have taken long to assemble. One example, a *denarius* hoard from Birdoswald fort, Cumbria, came complete with bronze arm purse (figure 1).

Contents of coin hoards

The hoard record from Roman Britain was shaped by certain factors: *selection* by individual hoarders; *legislation* (rarely recorded and usually inferred from evidence) favouring or outlawing certain coin types; *debasement* – changes in the economic relationship between the face value of a coin and its raw material, often a crucial factor in the breakdown of coinage systems; and the *supply* of coins to the island

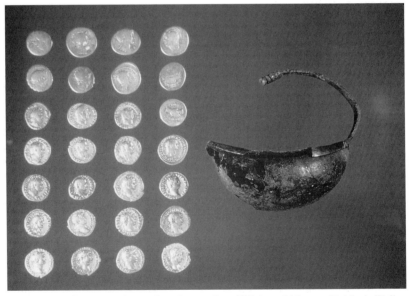

1. In 1949, during renovation work to the remains of Birdoswald fort on Hadrian's Wall, a bronze arm purse was discovered under a rampart backing. It contained twenty-eight *denarii* running up to the early years of Hadrian and was probably lost by a legionary engaged in construction work. (© Tullie House Museum)

(with the accompanying question of *monetisation* – how widespread was coin use). When we look at a hoard and wonder about its contents, we are trying to decide what combination of such factors was involved in its creation (and in some cases its abandonment).

While debasement and legislation will be examined alongside the appropriate evidence in the following chapters, the other two factors have more general features:

Selectivity

Hoarders apparently selected their coins to some extent, and denominations of precious and non-precious coins appear to have been largely kept separate. In some cases this is quite understandable. Gold and silver coins were handier forms of storing wealth than the comparable bulk of bronze coins, and changing from precious to base coins and *vice versa* usually incurred costs (of using money-changers). During the earlier empire, taxation had to be met in silver *denarii* and anyone who received income in *denarii* (for example the civil and military authorities, and those who traded with them) would probably have kept a store of silver and changed as little into bronze coins as possible. Up to the third century, hoards of *denarii* predominated over those of other metals and denominations.

Supply: evidence from the coin deposition at the Sacred Spring at Bath

Taking into account the patterns of the contents of as many hoards as possible shows something of the overall supply of Roman coinage to Britain. However, unlike hoards, which are deposits abandoned at one point in time, large groups of coins can also be found together because they were lost or abandoned by different people over a period of time – the 'back of the sofa' effect. A settlement site is the most common example, but there are also sites of habitual coin deposition, such as Coventina's Well at Carrawburgh on Hadrian's Wall, and the Sacred Spring of Sulis at Bath. Coins were deposited as such in order to attract the attention of a god or goddess – comparable with today's superstition of throwing coins into a fountain for good luck.

The Sacred Spring lies in what was once the south-east corner of the precinct of the temple of Sulis Minerva, one of the few classical Roman-style temples known in Britain. Deemed sacred to the goddess, the spring was developed as a place where worshippers could make offerings by throwing them into the water (figure 2). The 1970s excavations of the spring yielded personal items including gems, jewellery, tableware, and also more unusual objects, such as priestly regalia and even a washer from a Roman army catapult. Perhaps the most famous items are more than 1500 'curse tablets' – sheets of lead that were scratched with written communications to the divinity and then rolled up before

2. The Sacred Spring at Bath. Modern visitors have the same viewing access through the portals as the ancient worshippers, who deposited offerings through them. (Photograph: R. A. Abdy)

being tossed into the 'netherworld' beneath the spring. An extract from one example reads:

> I, Arminia, complain to you, Sulis, [that] you consume [i.e., destroy] Verecundinus [son of] Terentius, who has [stolen] two argentioloi from me.

This voice from the past mentions something called an '*argentiolos*' (= little silver). It is possibly a nickname for a silver *denarius* or *siliqua* (the latter would be particularly interesting since the name used nowadays is used in lieu of its so far unknown ancient name).

The Sacred Spring also contained 12,613 ancient coins, whose issues covered the whole Roman period in Britain. Activity reduced only in the second half of the fourth century, well into the period of Christian emperors; the conversion of rank-and-file pagans took many generations. Tossing coins into the spring seems to have been a regular occurrence, and the archaeologists at Bath were faced with the intriguing prospect of a large sample of coins deposited from the first century at the bottom of the pile, all the way up to those from the fifth century at the top – and the possibility that this could provide a model of the supply of Roman coins to Britain.

However, ancient operation of a sluice gate to clean the spring had mixed up its contents, invalidating the possibility of stratigraphical analysis and leaving a potentially distorted picture caused by the differing lengths of time coins spent in circulation before their deposition. They were therefore analysed (by D. R. Walker) according to when it was possible to have used the coins – the 'period of loss'. This is a picture derived from hoard studies (table from Walker, 1988):

Period of production	Period of loss	Total number of coins	Mean of coins deposited per annum
Before AD *c*.260	*c*.AD 60–260	7645	38.22
260–296	*c*.260–300	1902	47.55
294–353	*c*.294–353	2179	36.93
353–360	*c*.353–368	357	23.80
364–388	*c*.364–388	283	11.79
388–402	*c*.388–430	42	1.00

In order to compare different periods, the same level of activity over time had to be assumed (for example, ignoring the possibility that one visitor might throw in more than one coin or that a tariff of offerings that rose with inflation might have been in force). In fact, the average number of coins deposited per year remains fairly even until the mid fourth century. The activity levels at Bath contrast with Coventina's Well, which shows a significant drop in activity from the start of the later Roman empire, presumably reflecting the reduction in military manpower stationed on the frontiers (also indicated by the site-coin evidence at these forts and the changes to barrack blocks).

Calculations (using the mathematical relationship between the number of examples of a particular coin type present and the number of individual dies carved to produce them) performed on the Bath assemblage shows a degree of monetisation during early Roman Britain far lower than that in Italy. A highly monetised society (like modern Britain) will have a large physical amount of coins per person, in values down to the smallest unit, to enable anything to be bought and sold using money. An ancient, less monetised society might only have a limited range and total number of coins – usually high value, precious metal denominations. In such a society, most people would have to be self-sufficient peasantry, and low-value goods and services be repaid in kind (for example the exchange of commodities by barter). Like the economies they facilitate, monetisation is something that develops over time. The hoard chart (page 9) shows a general trend (however fluctuating) for more hoards over time (more hoards abandoned being an indicator of more hoarding activity) and thus an increasing number of coins among the people of Roman Britain. However, it should be remembered that what looks like Roman small change – in early Roman Britain this was effectively the copper *as* – still had a purchasing power far in excess of a modern penny. The cost of a haircut is recorded by chance as being one *as* – a service that would cost several pounds nowadays. For a sample of bronze coinage supplied to Britain in the middle of the second century, a total original-circulation value of about 10 million *sestertii* is estimated (one *sestertius* = four *asses*). In the context of a Roman Britain of perhaps 5 million people, this averages two *sestertii* per capita. Where does this place Roman Britain, with its otherwise relatively sophisticated range of coin denominations? It clearly had much more of a consumer society than, say, the sixth-century kingdoms of the Frankish and Visigothic barbarians who inherited much of the Roman west. The most likely economic 'landscape' is that Roman Britain, at least for the first couple of centuries, consisted of coin-using 'islands' of Roman military or civil (town-based) officialdom with their associated trading communities and native elites, in an overwhelming sea of virtually coinless peasants.

Supply: evidence for coin immobility in the Bath assemblage
Underlying the monetisation calculations is the idea of Britain as a closed 'coin province'. This applies particularly to the low denominations, which seem to have been shipped in bulk to the island never to circulate to another Roman province in any significant quantity. Because of this, the bronze denominations prior to *c*.260 show distinctive British period-patterns that would be impossible had such coins circulated unimpeded across the whole Western Roman Empire. Walker, in his study of the Bath assemblage, christened these periods:

> AD 43–95/6   'period of sporadic supply'
> AD 95/6–*c*.197   'period of regular supply'
> AD *c*.197–260   'period of minimal supply'

One-off shipments in the first period give way to annual supply in the second, no doubt helping to meet the needs of an economically maturing province. However, these virtually cease altogether *c*.197, with third-century Britain relying on recycled and increasingly worn coins of the first and second centuries until the breakdown of the early Roman system during the 270s. Of the great sporadic shipments – AD 64–7 (reign of Nero); 71–3, 77–8 (Vespasian); 86–7 (Domitian) – the first three came from the mint of Lyons (central France). By Domitian's reign, the Lyons mint had closed (to remain so until the later third century) and the supply route to Britain had to be extended to the mint of Rome. In any case, Rome was throughout this period the sole source of silver *denarii*, which, unlike bronze, had to be regularly supplied to Britain to meet state expenditure.

Supply: Roman Britain as a 'coin province'
Coins can be withdrawn to create hoards only from the material that

was available in circulation, and this in turn depended on what was shipped to the island (only very brief periods saw the production of Roman coins at British mints). So what does the Bath material imply about the character of coin circulation in Roman Britain? Once coins were supplied to Britain, they appear largely to have stayed on the island. The extent to which they did so is often argued over, but it is clear that coinage across the empire did not show uniform characteristics, indicating that stagnant 'pools' of circulation were the norm, rather than a completely free empire-wide mix. The AD 86–7 bronze shipment demonstrates this with particular force. Issues from the years 86–7 make up about 80 per cent or more of Domitian's bronze coins from the Sacred Spring and Coventina's Well. This is a similar pattern to hoard and site finds across Britain (their presence at Inchtuthil legionary base has helped date the first-century Roman abandonment of Scotland), but a marked contrast to the more even supply from throughout Domitian's rule (81–96) seen in evidence from Italy and the Rhine–Danube frontier.

When mints other than Rome supplied Britain, it is almost always the products of the nearest mints that predominate. This is most clearly seen in the bronzes of the second half of the first century, when the mint at Lyons was in operation, and in the explicitly mint-marked coins of the fourth century, when again mints in Gaul were operational and proved the most convenient suppliers. This detail also implies that coin hoards in Gaul should show many similar characteristics. That they do is an important point to bear in mind. Also important is the fact that coin hoards from beyond the frontier in Britain often show quite different characteristics (for example the Falkirk and Edston third-century *denarii* hoards from south-central Scotland show an adverse pattern of issues to their southern contemporaries), but it is beyond the scope of this book to explore these aspects further.

Even coinage that was periodically recalled as taxes – silver *denarii* in the earlier empire – often shows biases in circulation presence towards different areas of the empire (although the occasional exotic oddity suggests that it could circulate long distances – figure 15.4). How could such provincial patterns be maintained? A likely scenario was that the provincial finance minister (*procurator*) took receipt of the tax revenue. This was then immediately sent out again as payments for wages and other expenses for the military and civil service of the province. Britain, a relatively poor frontier province nevertheless housing one-tenth of the Roman army, would probably make a 'loss' and shortfalls would be topped up from the centre of the empire. In this way, any idiosyncrasies within the provincial circulation pool would perpetuate, leaving Britain as a distinctive 'coin province', whose changing features can be explored in the following chapters.

2
Early Roman hoards in Britain

The inhabitants of the lands that the Roman invaders first encountered, southern and eastern Britain, had long been familiar with using and hoarding coins. Features such as the classicising designs on late Celtic coins (figure 3) indicate that, prior to the invasion, southern Britain was already opening up to the Roman world and its ways. The coin-using Celts were quickly subdued by the Roman conquest of AD 43 and the early province took the form of an expanding central swath of Roman territory with peripheral native kingdoms of Roman allies: the Iceni, Regni and Brigantes. The victor, Claudius (AD 41–54), was keen to capitalise on his achievement by building a triumphal arch at Rome to link his name forever with such a famous victory, and this in turn was celebrated with a coin type (see figure 10.3). That expansion was seriously checked only

3. The Alton hoard from Hampshire, detected in 1996 alongside late Iron Age pottery, is a spectacular example of pre-Roman coinage in Britain: 256 gold staters of the local Atrebatic kings, deposited a couple of decades before the invasion of AD 43. Originally transmitted through the Celtic world from the Greeks, this size of gold piece was the preferred coin type in western pre-Roman Europe. Alton's latest coins show the transition from traditional Celtic to more classical styles (example inset of a stater of TINComarus, a Latin name meaning 'big fish'). Also illustrating the link to the classical world was the presence in the hoard of a Roman gold bracelet and a ring engraved with a dancing Maenad (an associate of the classical god Bacchus).

4. The Bredgar hoard from near Maidstone, Kent, discovered during building work in 1957. The coins had been neatly packed in rolls and, presumably, contained in a long-perished cloth or leather bag, and would have been a small, convenient size-to-value package for a highly mobile soldier campaigning in an unknown land. At the time, a basic legionary's salary was 225 *denarii* (nine *aurei*) a year – Bredgar's thirty-seven *aurei* would have been a very useful sum in an emergency.

by the Icenian revolt of AD 61 before the stabilisation of the British frontier (and a reduction of its army to fight elsewhere) in the late 80s.

The professional Roman army, with its regular wages, was heavily coin-dependent, and the new province immediately began using Roman money. It has been suggested that the Bredgar hoard (figure 4) might have been deposited for safety by a Roman officer during the invasion battles around the river Medway. Its thirty-seven gold *aurei* date from Julius Caesar, the first Roman to seek military adventure beyond the Channel, to those of Claudius. The AD 41–2 closing date is chronologically convenient but not (as so often with hoards) conclusive.

Although the *aureus* was the top denomination in the Roman coinage system and a particularly handy store of wealth for someone on the move – such as a merchant or soldier (for example Bredgar), the coin most used to pay imperial taxes was the silver *denarius*. A *denarius* was officially tariffed at sixteen copper *asses,* but the exchange rate would naturally vary (disadvantageously to the customer) if the services of a money-changer were involved. Even if they were not, buying goods in the market-place must have caused some sort of negotiation over the price with respect to the different coin proffered, since bronze was useful for small-scale purchases but silver was essential for longer-term obligations. Until the third century AD, the *denarius* was the favourite denomination for hoarding; bronze hoards tend to be fewer, and mixed

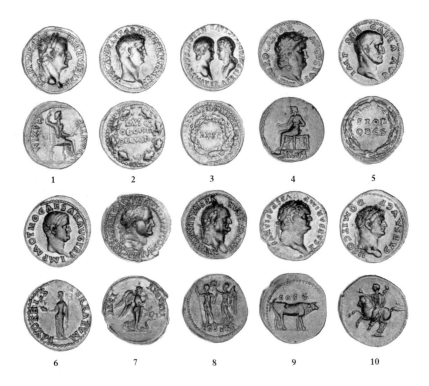

5. A selection from the 127 *aurei* (closing AD 78–9) detected in 1998 at Shillington, Bedfordshire. This hoard contains a substantial quantity of issues from before the Neronian reform (when the weight of the *aureus* was reduced), which are absent from later gold hoards such as Didcot and Corbridge discussed in the next chapter. (1) Tiberius, PONTIF MAXIM, RIC 29 (AD 14–37). (2) Claudius (oak-leaf crown), RIC 15 (AD 41–2). (3) Nero and Agrippina (titles around wreath), RIC 1 (AD 54). (4) Nero (Salus), RIC 66 (AD 64–8). (5) Galba, S P Q R / OB / C S, RIC 164 (AD 68–9). (6) Otho (Pax), RIC 3 (AD 69). (7) Vespasian (Nemesis), RIC 297 (AD 71). (8) Vespasian (Vespasian and Victory), RIC 105 (AD 77–8). (9) Vespasian for Titus (cow), RIC 188 (AD 76). (10) Vespasian for Domitian (Domitian riding), RIC 232 (AD 73). 1 was minted at Lyons, the rest at Rome.

silver-and-bronze hoards are rarer still. If one was lucky enough to receive payments in silver then the coins would no doubt be stored that way, and only what was needed for immediate spending would be changed down. If one received an income of bronze coins (through market-place takings, for example), one would no doubt eventually wish to acquire a store of silver for tax payment.

The Shillington hoard

Gold was particularly favoured for coinage in pre-Roman Britain and, indeed, Roman *aurei* may initially have been substitutes for the traditional use of Celtic gold coins for votive practices among the native civilians. It has been suggested that the Shillington hoard, Bedfordshire (figure 5), was a religious offering at a cult site. There were crop-marks at the site suggestive of a Romano-Celtic temple precinct and archaeological investigation revealed a civilian Romano-British site and much continuity with the pre-Roman, in the shape of late Iron Age and Roman coins and pottery. Temples traditionally offered a secure storage place for wealth in the classical world. However, in addition to the gold hoard, the presence and composition of a series of deposits of *denarii*, forming an unlikely hoard pattern, point to habitual coin-deposition without intention of recovery. There would be no reason why Roman coins would not be used for such a characteristically British ritual; the Roman-Celtic temple site at Wanborough, Surrey, has yielded more than a thousand Celtic and first-century AD Roman coins, and other native coin-deposition sites with continuity into the Roman period are beginning to be recognised.

Early *denarius* hoards

The earliest *denarius* hoards in Britain tend to cluster from around the young province's heartlands near the Thames estuary to a little beyond a line from the Wash to the Severn. They move out across Wales and the north only during the big Flavian-period advances of the AD 70s and 80s. Hoards buried in Claudian and early Neronian times can often look older than they are since they had a very good chance of not containing any new coins because of the paucity of silver produced from the time of Caligula (who closed the productive mint at Lyons, which had supplied the north-west since 15 BC) until Nero's reorganisation of the coinage in AD 64 (figure 6). Thus, a hoard containing only pre-Claudius coins does not indicate deposition before the invasion. There are around twice as many silver hoards closing with issues of Augustus, Tiberius and the Republic as those of Caligula, Claudius and the early years of Nero. Characteristically, Republican *denarii* continued circulating throughout the first century – even late-first-

1   2   3   4   5

6. The five *denarii* of the Owslebury hoard, metal-detected in 2001 in Hampshire, comfortably within the area of the earliest phase of the Roman province. Typically, aside from the worn state of the coins, the latest coin, AD 37, belies a Claudian or Neronian deposition date. (1) Republic, CN. LVCR TRIO (Castor and Pollux), RRC 237/1a (136 BC). (2) Republic, C. SERVEIL C.F. (two warriors), RRC 423/1 (57 BC). (3) Republic, T. CARISIVS (coin-minting tools), RRC 464/2 (46 BC). (4) Augustus (Gaius and Lucius Caesar), RIC 207 (7–6 BC). (5) Tiberius, PONTIF MAXIM, RIC 30 (AD 14–37). 4 and 5 were minted at Lyons, the rest at Rome.

7. The plough-scattered site of the Howe hoard from Norfolk has regularly produced finds since 1981. The hoard was an unusual mixture of gold and silver, but, taken separately, the 125 *denarii* and fifteen *aurei* (to AD 79) show typical circulation patterns.

and early-second-century hoards show a presence of 30 to 40 per cent. Although the hoarding habit was to keep the denominations separate, which reflects the problems with their exchangeability in everyday use, a few interesting mixed hoards are known from the first century, such as the Howe hoard from Norfolk (figure 7). Its 125 *denarii* to AD 87 show typical characteristics – 45 per cent Republican, a virtual hiatus from Caligula until the AD 64 reform, after which the run of issues extends up to the reign of Domitian. Gold coinage became much rarer in Britain after Celtic times (until the fourth century); nevertheless, because of the equally precious nature of gold, it was probably just as useful as silver when it was available. It is clear that in the early years of Roman Britain the end of native coin production did not immediately mean that it stopped being used. There are quite a number of hoards of worn Icenian silver units and more than half a dozen examples where, like Eriswell (figure 8), they are combined with early *denarii*. All occur within the territory of the Icenian kingdom and are good early evidence

8. The *denarii* of the Eriswell hoard from Norfolk (found on a building site in 1972) close with an unworn coin of AD 55. The rest of the seventy-two Roman coins are typical of a very early British *denarius* hoard (one-third are issues of Augustus and Tiberius, all but three of the rest Republican). The hoard also contained 255 Icenian silver units, much more worn than the latest Roman examples, suggesting that they had possibly ceased production around the time of the invasion but were nevertheless still in use into the late AD 50s.

of Roman coin use among the native population (Celtic coins being unlikely to be acceptable to the Romans). Furthermore, those containing *denarii* show that Icenian hoards all end before AD 61 – which suggests that their non-recovery could lie with the troubles of the Boudican revolt. Either they were lost by those who died in the fighting and subsequent persecutions, or perhaps they were forgotten in the wake of a demonetisation of Icenian coinage – possibly even before the absorption of the kingdom when Roman moneylenders were reportedly fuelling Icenian discontent.

Bronze hoards

Early Roman bronze coins are more closely linked to the army (having a greater presence on early military sites than civil settlements). This suggests that it took time for monetisation to develop and perhaps also for many native Britons to become accustomed to using coins not backed by the intrinsic value of a precious metal content. Although very restricted in area of usage, Celtic bronze coins were beginning to catch on just before the invasion. Indeed, there is an unusual example of a mixed Roman and Celtic bronze hoard from Timsbury, Hampshire, found in 1907 in an Iron Age 'Hod Hill type' pot. The forty-three Roman bronzes, closing AD *c*.90 (mainly *asses,* but including a *sestertius*), were accompanied by eighteen Durotrigan 'uninscribed' bronzes. On the whole, first-century bronze hoards tend to be small assemblages (usually under thirty coins). Being hoarded in such small amounts gives the impression that they were stores of ready cash. Soldiers needed bronze coins only for pocket money, and while they were the only users in Britain there was probably not the same need to supply bronze as regularly as the silver *denarius*. Kempsford, Gloucestershire (figure 9), is a typical early bronze hoard of six *dupondii* and twenty-one *asses* to AD 87 (not including four later strays). Like the Sacred Spring coins, this hoard shows groups typical of the bronze coins supplied to Britain throughout the first century: AD 64–7, 71–3, 77–8 (Lyons mint); and AD 86–7 (from Rome).

Claudian copies

Unmistakably illegal forgery, intending to deceive and swindle, occurred right from the start of Roman Britain (figure 10). However, three coins of Claudius in the Kempsford hoard illustrate the peculiar conditions facing the earliest Roman bronze coins circulating in Britain. The invading troops would have brought bronze with them, but then supplies dried up because of a production gap during later Claudian and early Neronian times, until the resumption of production in AD 64 and the reopening of the Lyons mint. Instead, old bronzes were recycled,

9. A selection of bronze *asses* from the Kempsford hoard, found beside the river Thames in 1978. (1) 'Claudius' (Minerva), copy. (2) Nero (Victory), RIC 477 (AD 64–7). (3) 'Nero' (Victory), copy. (4) Vespasian (eagle), RIC 747 (AD 72–3). (5) Titus (Spes), RIC 786 (AD 77–8). (6) Domitian (Fortuna), RIC 353a (AD 87). 2, 4 and 5 were minted at Lyons, 6 at Rome. (© Ashmolean Museum)

10. A selection from the 110 silver-plated *denarius* forgeries (silver foil covering a base-metal core) of the North Suffolk hoard, found by metal detector in 1995. They copy official types of up to AD 51. 'Claudius', (1) (Constantia); (2) (Nemesis); (3) DE BRITANN (Claudius's triumphal arch at Rome). (Numbers 2 and 3 share the same obverse die. The number of unworn coins struck from the same dies shows that they had never been circulated since it would be highly improbable that so many die-identical coins could be subsequently reunited in a single deposit. This strongly incriminates the hoarder as also being the forger.

and, if especially worn, they could be countermarked to show official approval. Additionally, Britain had not yet built up the circulation pool that would see it through the bronze 'famine' to come during the early third century, and a feature of the bronzes of this period is the mass production of copies (the first of three forging 'epidemics' that also affect the silver-bronze coinage of the late third and early fourth centuries). Copies form such a significant presence in the British and Gaulish circulation (and as finds on military sites) that it is plausible either that they were made for the army, or that the authorities tolerated their creation by private enterprise (although a single copy of a Nero bronze in Kempsford shows that the tradition carried on beyond the supply crisis). For most Claudian copies the model was the first issue of Claudius's bronze (which lacks the title *pater patriae* ['P P'], 'father of the fatherland'), but it is clear that copies were in turn copied, as they can be sorted in declining size and diverging style from the original. The relatively good Kempsford copies show that, although the worst specimens might have been put aside upon the reappearance of good coin, the better examples continued in use (sometimes countermarked) despite the poor quality of their designs compared to the later first-century official coins.

3
The age of silver: *denarius*-based coinage in Britain during the second and third centuries

In the second century the limits of the province crystallised, and it received a second visit from a reigning emperor, Hadrian, in 121–2. Britain also began to mature economically, with grand civic building projects flourishing in a way that would not be repeated in later periods. The frontier briefly moved northwards from Hadrian's Wall, and the Antonine frontier, 142–*c*.169, was created. The Britannia type of 154–5 may indicate trouble on this new frontier, while a victory concluding a war in 184 is recorded on coins of Commodus (figure 11). This appears to have been a hard-fought war (Dio Cassius 73, 8). There is a peak number (nearly one hundred) of mostly smallish hoards (around one

| 1 | 2 | 3 |

11. The Roman conquest gives way to defence of Roman assets. Antoninus Pius's Britannia *sestertius* of 143 shows the province perched proudly on a representation of the new Antonine Wall (1). However, the slumped, disconcerted Britannia on his *dupondius* and *as* type of 154–5 suggests things had gone awry (2). The 184 Victory recorded on a *sestertius* of Commodus was not won through conquest of territory, but in response to barbarian attack (3).

hundred coins or fewer) in Britain, closing with Commodus's father, Marcus Aurelius (161–80). Events in Britain might have been in the form of a protracted disturbance, flaring up two or three times throughout Marcus's reign, and outbreaks of plague – as implied by historical sources (for example Dio Cassius 61, 16). The timing seems about right to suggest that the peak of unrecovered hoards under Marcus might have been the result, however indirect, of barbarian activity that was not finally settled until the early 180s.

In the second century and the first half of the third, the silver *denarius*

12. The strongroom of the fort of Chesters on Hadrian's Wall. Soldiers could also keep a store of money closer to hand, as was shown by the excavation of three hoards from beneath barracks at the Second Legion's base at Caerleon. (Photograph: R. A. Abdy)

continued to be the backbone of the Roman currency system and, together with gold and bronze, was usually produced at Rome. Throughout most of the second century, up to the reign of Septimius Severus (193–211), a legionary's basic pay was 300 *denarii* per year – before stoppages for food, equipment and other expenses. Soldiers would take receipt of the remaining money at thrice-annual pay parades, using the facilities in their fort's headquarters as a bank (figure 12).

A survey of British hoards closing with coins of Hadrian (117–38) will show the formation of characteristics typical of the later *denarius* circulation. For example, the Birdoswald purse hoard (figure 1) contains one coin of Hadrian from near the beginning of his reign and also seven from the Republic, more than a century and a half earlier. In subsequent hoards closing with Antoninus Pius (138–61), all pre-AD 64 coins appear to be absent from circulation. AD 64 was the year that the weight of the *denarius* decreased from 84 to 96 to the (Roman) pound (accompanied by a small drop in silver purity from around 98 to 93 per cent), making earlier coins more valuable as a raw material.

Coins ripe for profitable reuse would have been very easy to spot: issues of the Republic; the first four emperors; and the early issues of Nero, which invariably employed a bare-headed image, his wreathed images effectively marking out the debased coins. The exception to these disappearing coins are Mark Antony's legionary issues, struck to commemorate his legions just before his defeat at the battle of Actium in 31 BC. Initial survival of the legionary *denarii* was due no doubt to their impure alloy, which was more debased than the late silver of Nero. However, they maintain a strong presence in British hoards until almost the end of the *denarius* period, and it is clear that, when very worn, they were the one type overlooked for removal from circulation even when later coins of similar purity did begin to disappear. There was ancient suspicion over the quality of Antony's coins, but whether this was the sole reason, or whether people had acquired the habit of cherry-picking circulating coins (for example by recognising imperial portraits – Republican coins having long disappeared by the middle of the second century), is not entirely clear. Likewise, by the middle of the second century, all of the purer silver of Domitian (who began a short-lived attempt to restore the *denarius* to pre-64 standards) begins to vanish, leaving behind the coins of his father and older brother (which contain about 91 per cent silver).

Lawrence Weston, from Bristol, is a typical *denarius* hoard closing in the 150s. Found in 1988 in the front garden of a suburban house, it consisted of 598 coins originally covered by a sandstone slab (possibly once a Roman roof-tile). On a graph it shows a typical pattern: no coins

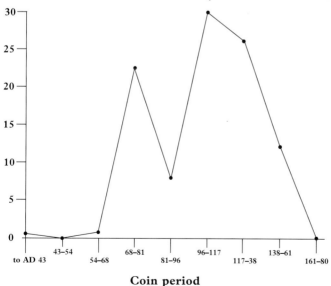

The Lawrence Weston hoard (958 denarii to AD 157)

Coin period

prior to Nero with the exception of legionary *denarii*; a peak for Vespasian (AD 68–81); and a dip for Domitian (AD 81–96). The second-century coins show a more natural circulation presence, with coins of Trajan and Hadrian at their peak and those of Pius yet to flood fully into circulation.

Where do the missing coins go? State recoinage is the obvious answer – using the old, purer silver coin recovered in taxes to produce a greater number of new debased issues. However, this is not the only factor at work: individuals, too, could exploit the additional bullion value of older coins during times of debasement. The process is shown in a very unusual hoard from Snettisham, Norfolk, which contained all the materials needed for a Roman jeweller to carry out his trade (figure 13). It contained bronze coins forming a normal modest bronze hoard of the mid second century – probably the jeweller's petty cash. The silver coins, however, were clearly being used for quite a different purpose and were at odds with other contemporary *denarius* hoards such as Lawrence Weston. Seventy-four coins (nearly 90 per cent pure) belonged to the reign of Domitian alone. In terms of silver purity, his coin issues

13. The Snettisham jeweller's hoard, discovered during house construction in a residential street in 1985. In a locally produced coarse-ware pot was a varied collection of jewellery, twenty-seven bronze coins and eighty-three *denarii*, to 154–5. Conditions of burial were so good that even pieces of Roman cloth were found. Some of the jewellery items were in a scrap or unfinished condition, for example rings lacking their stone insets or wire clasps detached from necklaces, and there was a large collection of 110 loose gems saved for remounting. In addition, there were silver ingots and a burnishing tool. Inset: one of the seventy-four Domitian *denarii* intended for the melting pot (Minerva reverse, RIC 188, AD 95).

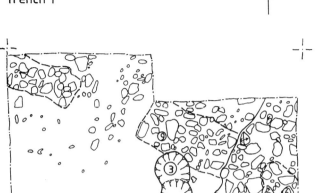

14. The pit (H) containing the Shapwick hoard in the corner of the back room of the villa. (Courtesy of the excavator, R. Brunning)

can be divided into three periods: AD 81–2 (91 per cent – prior to the increase); 82–5 (98 per cent); and 85–96 (93.5 per cent). Coins of the first period were avoided, along with those of the earlier Flavian emperors that had similar silver levels; the Snettisham hoarder had deliberately selected all his coins from the third period. Contemporary hoard evidence would suggest that all of the purest 'second phase' Domitian coins were already removed from circulation by the early second century – long before the time of this hoarder. Our jeweller had therefore selected the coins with the most bullion available to him at the time to use as raw material – some of which had already been turned into ingot form. There must have been many like him – whether jewellers, currency speculators or even forgers – all helping to drive the finer silver coins from circulation, and all part of the process behind the old saying 'Bad money drives out the good' (Gresham's Law).

The Shapwick Villa hoard

The largest and most typical *denarius* hoard of the period is the

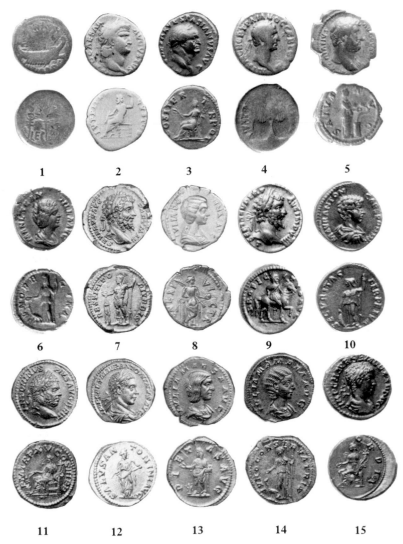

15. A selection of the Shapwick Villa *denarii*. (1) Mark Antony (galley and standards), RRC 544 (31 BC). (2) Nero (Jupiter), RIC 53 (AD 65). (3) Vespasian (Pax), RIC 10 (AD 69–70). (4) Trajan, silver *drachm* (two lyres) (AD 98–99). (5) Hadrian (Salus), RIC 267 (134–8). (6) Manlia Scantilla (Juno), RIC 7 (193). (7) Severus (Severus sacrificing), RIC 167 (200–1). (8) Julia Domna (Venus), RIC— (193–4). (9) Severus (Severus riding), RIC 494 (197). (10) Caracalla (Minerva), RIC 330 (*c*.196-7). (11) Caracalla (Annona), RIC 195 (212). (12) Elagabalus (Salus), RIC 140 (218–22). (13) Julia Maesa (Pietas), RIC 263 (218–22). (14) Julia Mamaea (Juno), RIC 343 (222). (15) Severus Alexander (Concordia), RIC 275 (223). All mint of Rome except 1 (mobile mint); 4 (Lycia); 8 (Alexandria); 9, 10 and 15 (eastern).

Shapwick Villa treasure from Somerset: at 9213 coins, the largest (by a factor of three) found in Britain; discovered in 1998 (see figure 43). Found with the aid of a metal detector, the undisturbed portion lay in a pit whose rounded but irregular shape suggested that the coins were originally contained in some sort of leather or textile sack, long decomposed. The coins were found in neat rows – perhaps once wrapped in individual piles. Geophysical survey revealed the site to be within a grand villa complex (65 by 45 metres), the find itself concealed in a corner of a small (5 by 3 metres) back room (figure 14). For a major hoard, such an important context was completely unprecedented and allows more speculation about its purpose than most other cases. The hoard was almost certainly buried during occupation of the villa, and its location in a private back room strongly suggests that it was the villa treasury. (Interestingly, at Frocester Court Roman villa in Gloucestershire a small back room was excavated during the 1960s and found to contain the remains of an iron-bound strongbox sunk into the floor. This was interpreted as the villa's office, where business transactions could be made, workers paid and the liquid assets of the villa safely stored.)

The Shapwick coins close in 224 and form a useful sample of the circulating *denarius* population around that time (figure 15) – the next step in the circulation history after Lawrence Weston. The Antony legionary issues, the only coins earlier than AD 64, are still present in quantity but nearly worn to blank discs (figure 15.1). Coins of the first and early second centuries had also become quite worn by the time of their abandonment in the Shapwick hoard. But wear is never an exact process; for example figure 15.2,3 shows a typically worn example of Nero alongside a comparatively unworn Vespasian – both having circulated for about a century and a half. The hoard as a whole shows two distinct sections. All the coins prior to 193 show similar proportions to the plethora of British hoards ending in coins of the Antonine emperors. These are dwarfed, however, by the coins of Severus and his successors, which make up 75 per cent of the total. The reason for this was the great debasement of 194–5, in which the *denarius* – which had been slowly dropping in fineness during the second century – was reduced to barely more than 50 per cent silver. Severus had doubled the army pay rates (to a basic legionary salary of 600 *denarii*) as part of his bid for power, and debasement helped boost new production – the effect appearing as a dam burst in the hoard record. New supplies to Britain of the lower-value bronze coins dry up at this point and the *denarius*, declining in value, seems to begin to fulfil lower transactional functions, heralding the monetary character of later periods.

There is another reason for the dominance of Severan issues in late

32

16. Despite its doubtful outcome, 'Victory in Britain' was recorded on Severus's coins – such as this *denarius* (x1.5) from Shapwick minted for Geta (RIC 91), Severus's second son and co-emperor (208–11).

denarius hoards in Britain. From 208, until his death in 211, the aged emperor mounted his last military adventure in Britain (figure 16), taking with him 'an immense amount of money' (Dio 77, 11), much of which must have found its way into the British circulation. A particular feature of Severan *denarii* is two or three groups that appear on stylistic grounds to have been produced in Syria and Egypt (for example figure 15.8 shows a similar style to contemporary Alexandrian tetradrachms). With the exception of the Severan issues, coins from the eastern empire are rarely found in Britain in the *denarius* period, but there are some remarkable examples in the Shapwick hoard. There are three from the province of Lycia (in Asia Minor) minted during the reign of Trajan (figure 15.4) and a Severan-period coin from Caesarea in Cappadocia. They are not *denarii* but *drachmae* with Greek legends, but they were superficially similar enough – in size, weight and appearance – to have been accepted in circulation, and they have been found occasionally in other hoards, and also as site finds (for example at the fort of Camelon near the Antonine Wall, exactly the opposite end of the Roman world to their origin). There is a handful of *denarii* outside the reign of Severus that can also be attributed to mints in the east of the empire (in Shapwick there are examples of Hadrian, Elagabalus and Severus Alexander). However, what makes the eastern Severan *denarii* different is that they begin to appear in significant quantity about the time of the British campaigns (a dozen or more years after their production, which flourished in 193-7 but had died out by 202). Additionally, over the course of the third century they continue to increase proportionally in comparison with the contemporary issues of the mint of Rome. This is seen by analysing hoards with successively later terminal dates. They show that the presence of eastern *denarii* (e.g. figure 15.8–10) in the Romano-British circulation remains low during the lifetimes of Severus and Caracalla. However, by the 270s (represented by hoards from the end of the *denarius* period such as M1, described below) 50 per cent of the surviving silver minted between 193 and 197 appears to be of Middle Eastern origin.

There are two theories to explain this – 'spread' or 'shrinkage'. Either the eastern issues spread in from the continent and mixed with the British circulation pool (contrary to the immobile picture of an isolated

17. The discovery made by a digger-operator who worked on the Leicestershire stretch of the M1, but who died before he could divulge its findspot.

island province from the Sacred Spring coins), or their numbers remained steady in the British coin population, once introduced during the Severan campaigns, while the mint of Rome examples subsequently shrunk by being removed in response to debasement. The latter theory would connect coins from hoards such as Shapwick with the war chest of Severus – only the third emperor to visit Britain, but the last to attempt to conquer the whole of the island.

The final stages of the *denarius* are demonstrated by the 'M1 Motorway' hoard, closing in 270 (figure 17). Of the 435 coins in the hoard, just less than half are *denarii* and the rest radiates – the *denarius*-multiple introduced in 215, which, after a false start, began to take over as the main denomination in the reign of Gordian III (238–44). It was another form of debasement, since despite probably being a double-*denarius*, it used only one and a half times the amount of silver. Alongside the *denarius*, the radiate also declined in silver content until the nadir of around 270 (figure 18). British hoards with a significant component of *denarii* closing after 260 are quite unusual and contain widely varying proportions of issues. This indicates rapid and traumatic changes to the coinage at this time. Debasement continued to displace earlier silver coins at an ever-increasing rate: in the M1 hoard, with the exception of

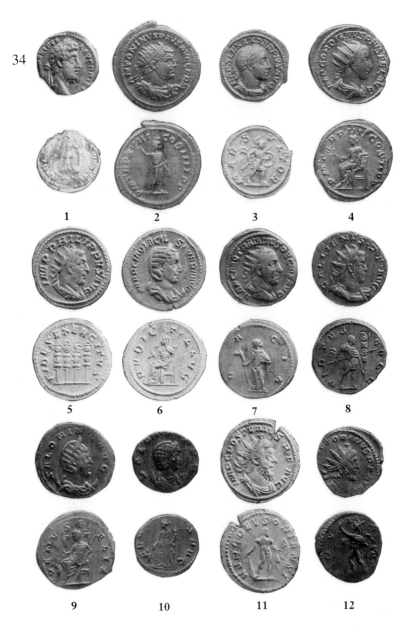

18. A selection from the M1 hoard. The radiates (all except 1 and 3, which are *denarii*) chart the decline from a 5 gram base-silver alloy of about 50 per cent fine to scruffy silvered bronze barely 2 grams and less than 5 per cent silver. (1) Commodus (Apollo), RIC 218 (191). (2) Caracalla (Serapis), RIC 263 (215). (3) Severus Alexander (Mars), RIC 246 (232). (4) Gordian III (Apollo), RIC 88 (241). (5) Philip I (army standards), RIC 62 (247–9). (6) Otacilia (Pudicitia), RIC 123c (244–6). (7) Decius (province of Dacia), RIC 12b (249–51). (8) Gallienus (Virtus/Gallienus), RIC 58 (257–8). (9) Salonina (Venus), RIC 7 (253–60). (10) Salonina (Fecunditas), RIC cf. 5 (266). (11) Postumus (Hercules), RIC 64 (261). (12) Victorinus (Sol), RIC 113 (269). (All mint of Rome except 8, 9, 11 and 12, which were minted in Gaul.)

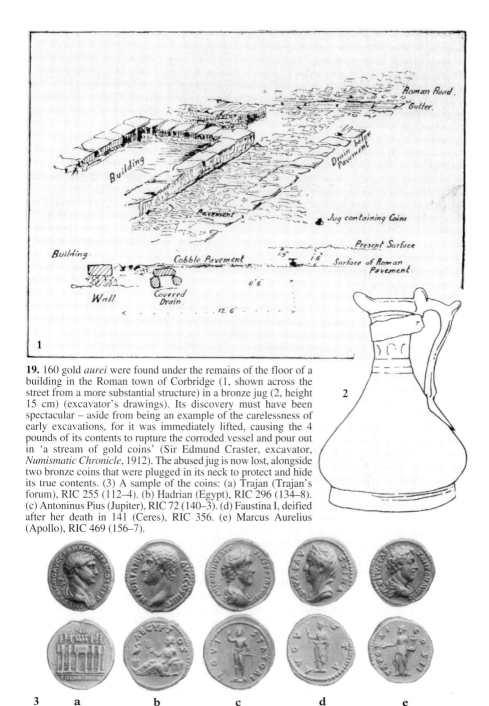

19. 160 gold *aurei* were found under the remains of the floor of a building in the Roman town of Corbridge (1, shown across the street from a more substantial structure) in a bronze jug (2, height 15 cm) (excavator's drawings). Its discovery must have been spectacular – aside from being an example of the carelessness of early excavations, for it was immediately lifted, causing the 4 pounds of its contents to rupture the corroded vessel and pour out in 'a stream of gold coins' (Sir Edmund Craster, excavator, *Numismatic Chronicle*, 1912). The abused jug is now lost, alongside two bronze coins that were plugged in its neck to protect and hide its true contents. (3) A sample of the coins: (a) Trajan (Trajan's forum), RIC 255 (112–4). (b) Hadrian (Egypt), RIC 296 (134–8). (c) Antoninus Pius (Jupiter), RIC 72 (140–3). (d) Faustina I, deified after her death in 141 (Ceres), RIC 356. (e) Marcus Aurelius (Apollo), RIC 469 (156–7).

3 a   b   c   d   e

a solitary Commodus (figure 18.1), all pre-Severan coins – even the Antony legionary *denarii* – had disappeared. The M1 hoard represents the last grab of (relatively) good silver coins just as virtual bronze coins with the same face value were being produced, changing the Roman coinage system beyond recognition.

Other hoards: gold

Gold hoards are always rare, and especially from the first to the third century (much more so than in the late pre-Roman Iron Age or the fourth to the early fifth century), but this period does contain three recorded examples. There were 160 *aurei* found at Corbridge, Northumberland, during excavations in 1911 (figure 19); next came Didcot in Oxfordshire, closing, like Corbridge, in 160 (figure 20); and forty-three *aurei* (to *c.*180) were discovered during excavations at Plantation Place, in the City of London, in 2000. The last hoard was hidden in a long-decayed bag under the floor of a substantial house. With the house inhabited for at least a century after the hoard was

20. Didcot (Oxfordshire), a metal-detector find from 1995 consisting of 126 gold *aurei* and the remains of their Oxfordshire coarse-ware pot.

21. The Curridge hoard, found by metal detector in 1998, comprises 425 worn bronze coins to 209, all *sestertii* with the exceptions of six *dupondii* or *asses*. It had been held in a large coarse-ware jar and a fine samian dish (made in central Gaul around 150–90), which had probably been used as a makeshift lid.

abandoned, it appears that its subsequent occupants remained unaware of the riches beneath their feet. In terms of composition, pre-AD 64 and Domitianic *aurei* are largely absent for similar reasons to *denarius* hoards, although in the case of gold, reduction in the value of the coin occurs through weight decrease rather than metal dilution.

Other hoards: bronze

On a weight-to-value basis, large, low-value bronze coins are not such a convenient store of funds as silver or gold coins. This appears to be reflected in the selective nature of hoarding: bronze hoards make up less than 15 per cent of second- and early to mid third-century hoard cases and only a handful comprise over one hundred coins (although this figure may be artificially low, since there was no requirement to report finds of bronze coins until 1997).

A good example of this type of hoard is Curridge from Berkshire (figure 21). During the late second century, bronze production began to be cut back in favour of silver, and for the final phase of this coinage (up to its discontinuation in the 260s) very few third-century issues reached Britain, reused first- and second-century bronzes making up the bulk of the circulation. This makes small and medium-size bronze hoards whose issues run up to the end of the second century (such as Curridge) quite difficult to date. Nor is wear (always a subjective quality on coins) much use as an indicator, since the usual degree of wear is very high anyway (in the same way that today's lowest-value banknotes wear out long before the higher ones, Roman small change was worked harder in circulation than silver and gold). In the Curridge hoard, the sequence of issues tails off sharply with only six Severan coins. This simply shows that deposition occurred sometime after the supply of new bronze (of Severan and later periods) was choked off, rather than being a firm indicator that the coins were abandoned before new issues reached the hoarder – as would normally be the case with a contemporary *denarius* hoard. We can be reasonably certain that Shapwick, because of its great size and its termination during a period of regularly supplied *denarii*, was abandoned very shortly after 224. Curridge, however, could still have been in use any time up to about 260, before old *sestertii*

22. The usurper Postumus's (260–9) innovative method of using recycled second-century bronzes. The coin has his image struck over that of an Antonine emperor, 161–92. (The name ANTONINVS can still be seen between 8 o'clock and 11 o'clock.)

overstruck with new dies made a brief appearance (figure 22). Indeed, if Curridge had been smaller than 425 coins, the six Severan examples might not have been present, leaving the impression of an even earlier hoard, while if it were larger, it might well have contained examples of scarce mid third-century issues. For example, at 1037 bronzes, the Gare hoard from Cornwall (discovered during agricultural work in 1967) is more than twice as big. In addition, it contains forty-seven *denarii* and radiates down to 270. It contains only twenty-five post-Severan *sestertii* (2.4 per cent), down to the last examples of the denomination of c.260–1. However, over the rest of the hoard the distribution of issues looked similar to Curridge, with the earliest coins dating to the Flavians but being mostly made up of coins of the reigns of Trajan, Hadrian and the Antonines.

The Gare hoard suggests that the largest bronze hoards occur at the very end of the period of use of the *sestertius* and its fractions (*dupondii* and *asses*). Possibly a number of substantial hoards were abandoned because inflation had rendered them worthless or they had been demonetised, since their intrinsic value had overtaken that of the higher-denomination silvered-bronze coins (perhaps being a parallel to the giant radiate hoards discussed in the next chapter).

A final point is that both Gare and Curridge are composed almost entirely of *sestertii*, rather than fractions. This is typical of the later second and the third century (around 80 per cent of bronze hoards from Marcus Aurelius to the 270s listed in the Robertson corpus are mainly *sestertii*) and is a reversal of the first-century situation, in which only about 16 per cent of bronze hoards have *sestertii* as the dominant denomination. While this might reflect the selectivity of hoarders, the evidence of the Bath assemblage (where any bias could be expected to be towards lower denominations) confirms the dominance of the *sestertius* among bronzes of the late second to the third century. This is a stock theme for Roman coins in Britain: a steady shift of emphasis to a higher denomination as the lower ones become less viable to produce, or at least to transport long distances. From the 270s, the *sestertius* and its fractions, like the *denarius*, had been driven out of circulation. They had become more valuable as raw materials – probably not least for the sinister purpose of helping to make radiate copies (a typical early *as* of around 10 grams could furnish, especially with additional alloying with cheap lead, the metal to make several 2–3 gram radiate copies all of higher potential face value). *Sestertii* and *dupondii* made of *orichalcum* (an attractive brassy alloy of copper and zinc) could find such uses as inlaying on late Roman bronze and ironwork. All that went before was swept away by the radiate, which had itself become virtually a bronze coin, the logical conclusion of the downward spiral of coinage debasement.

4
The age of debased silver and extreme hoarding in Roman Britain

During the troubled third century, Britain formed part of the Gallic usurpation zone (260–74) and was a heavy user of the coinage produced by its rebel emperors. Barely more than a decade after its return to central rule, the island became the centre of a new usurpation under Carausius (287–93) and Allectus (293–6). In 306, Constantius I, who had defeated Allectus, followed Severus and became the second emperor to die at York while on campaign; his son Constantine I ('the Great') (306–37) succeeded him on the spot. Constantine's son and successor in the west, Constans I (337–50) was the last legitimate emperor to visit Britain, but his reign was cut short by Magnentius (350–3). The latter remained a usurper, although his war with Constans's brother Constantius II (337–61) was closely fought. In the aftermath, the influential classes of Romano-British society who had supported the usurper were severely persecuted. It seems to be more than coincidence that the great villas that had flourished during the early fourth century – havens for the wealthy elite from high-maintenance cities – begin to show decline in number and extent after this point.

For almost a century (260s–350s), the coinage is a complicated and unstable mix of types, reforms and weight reductions and is covered in detail by Casey (1980). However, as far as Roman Britain was concerned there were only two significant denominations, both made from silvered bronze: the debased radiate; and its successor, the *nummus*, which replaced it when Britain returned to the imperial fold in 296. Both were multiples (the radiate possibly a double) of the old *denarius*, now a notional unit in which prices were expressed. Just exactly how many *denarii* they represented is still a subject of debate, but their face value was subject to change, and it is clear from surviving records, such as papyri from Egypt, that the spending power of the notional *denarius* was relentlessly shrinking in relation to the services and goods that it could purchase. By 301, a labourer might receive twenty-five *denarii* for a day's work (as opposed to one *denarius* in the first and second centuries); and one hundred *denarii* should have been able to purchase a standard measure of wheat (once less than a *denarius* in the first century). The alternative to the silvered-bronze radiate was the gold *aureus*, but for this period these are virtually non-existent in Britain. (The *aureus* had effectively lost any face value and was priced by weight.)

By the 270s coin portraits began to look distinctly post-classical.

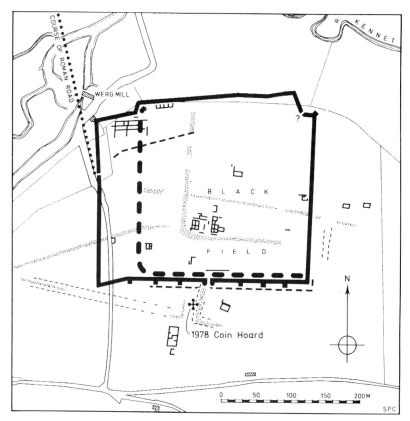

23. A plan of the Roman town of Cunetio and the hoard findspot. (Excavator's drawing)

Rendered with an incorporeal economy of line, emperors' images generally followed the iconic styles initially of Diocletian (284–305) and thereafter of Constantine. With the complete debasement of the radiates – driven by inflation to very high-volume production – issues consisted only of repetitive stock reverses, at times struck on rather scruffy blanks (explicit historical references, such as in figures 11 and 16, had largely ceased). By the fourth century, imagery could be quite schematic (for example giant emperor subjugating tiny foe and such like). Coins bore simpler forms of imperial title and as a medium relied on the bluntest visual messages.

Debased radiates: the Cunetio treasure

Since its discovery in 1978 at Mildenhall in Wiltshire, near the Roman

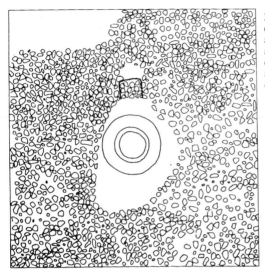

24. The Cunetio hoard coins were concealed within two containers: a now fragmentary lead box; and a large, locally made 'Savernake' coarse-ware storage jar over half a metre wide. (Excavator's drawings)

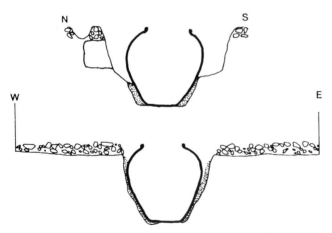

small town that gave it its name, the Cunetio hoard of 54,951 coins remains the biggest Roman hoard ever found in Britain (figure 23). It is surpassed only by a handful of other hoards found in the whole of the Roman Empire, such as the Réka-Devnia hoard from Bulgaria (81,044 *denarii* and radiates to *c*.250), the largest published Roman hoard ever found. Even this is eclipsed if reports of two unpublished debased-radiate hoards are to be believed; Évreux in France and Komin in Yugoslavia may have had over 100,000 and 300,000 coins respectively. However, although Cunetio is remarkable for its extreme size, it is an

25. A selection of debased radiates from Cunetio and the Tinwell hoards (2830 coins, to 275, found in Rutland, together with a Nene Valley ware pot, by a detectorist in 1999). Tinwell's 996 radiate copies show a bewildering array, with the wilder styles and diminished sizes from the prototypes marking out later generations of copies. (1) An official Spes type of Tetricus I, RIC 136 (270–4), from Cunetio, and (1a–c) irregular versions from Tinwell. (2) An official priest's implements type of Tetricus II, RIC 258 (270–4), from Cunetio, and (2a–d) irregular versions from Tinwell.

extremely common type of hoard. There are well over two hundred known hoards in Britain that close with the end of the Gallic Empire (274) or that sometimes include tiny numbers of coins of the reunited empire, up to 294. The reason probably lies with the improved style of radiate introduced by Aurelian in 274 (figure 27.1). A hypothetical demonetisation by Aurelian may have enforced these as the only radiates allowed to circulate or made the exchange of old radiates impracticable or just not worthwhile.

Cunetio closes with coins of Tetricus I and II (270–4), father and son, who were the last rulers of the breakaway 'Gallic Empire', figure 25.1,2. Although the finders completely mixed up the coins, it appears that the two containers (figure 24) may have had different deposition dates (perhaps one container becoming full and closed off while the other was filled) but that the overwhelming majority was deposited in the early 270s.

Cunetio represents the next stage on from the M1 hoard. During the 260s, complete debasement had occurred much earlier in the territory of the central empire controlled by Gallienus, about 260 (figure 18.10). However, in the areas using Gallic usurpers' coinage, debased sole-rule Gallienus coins (and those in the name of his empress, Salonina) had hardly penetrated the circulation before 268, when Gallic standards dropped to the same level (figures 18.12; 25.1,2), but as a result of this debasement (and probably helped by reunification by 274) they could now flood in. The M1 hoard, closing 270, had sole-reign Gallienus (260–8) to Postumus in a ratio of 1:12; in Cunetio – just four years later – the debased Gallienus outnumbered Postumus, which by then had become attractive for removal to recoup their excess silver. Like M1, Cunetio also contained *denarii* stretching back to the reign of Commodus (there was also a single *sestertius* of Domitian present) but although they numbered just over 600 coins, this represents only around 1 per cent of the hoard. Indeed, all coins prior to 253 made up just over 5 per cent of Cunetio, and completely debased issues had effectively eclipsed everything else in circulation.

Normanby and Blackmoor

The evidence of the second- and third-biggest hoards from Roman Britain has served to complicate the pre-Aurelian radiate demonetisation theory. In 1985 a hoard of 47,912 radiates was discovered at Normanby in Lincolnshire, again contained in a large Romano-British storage jar. Again, with the exception of its size, most of the hoard is unremarkable and consists almost entirely of debased radiates from the central empire throughout the 260s and the Gallic Empire from the late 260s and the early 270s. However, what caused most interest at the time was that it ran up to coins of 289, early in the reign of the British usurper Carausius. This sequence was taken later still by the Blackmoor hoard, which comprised nearly 30,000 radiates to the reign of Allectus (293–6). Unlike its two fellow giants, which were both found with metal detectors, Blackmoor was unearthed by agricultural work on the Earl of Selborne's Hampshire estate in 1873. The coins, in their two giant pots (see page 3), remained at the estate as curiosities for many years, the Earl's more interested guests being allowed to pick handfuls to take as souvenirs. It was sold off by his descendants in 1975, when it was examined at The British Museum. Similar to Normanby in that it consists mainly of the debased radiates, it also contains around 600 coins of the Britannic Empire (284–96), the largest number of coins from any recorded hoard of Carausius.

Both Normanby and Blackmoor show the development of Carausian coinage. A series of early issues carries no mint markings and is of a crudely expressive style, many showing similarities to the work of engravers of radiate copies, whose locally available talents Carausius presumably employed (figure 27.5). These make up the majority of both hoards (54 out of 73 for Normanby and 260 out of 546 for Blackmoor). However, the later Blackmoor hoard also shows significant numbers of the developed Carausian system, the first Roman-style coins with British mint marks: the London 'ML' mint (figure 27.6); the 'C' mint (figure 27.7) (hoard distribution evidence suggests a western source, Cirencester or Gloucester being possibilities); the rarer 'RSR' mint (possibly a special court mint mainly dealing with imperial monetary gifts and bonuses); and another, unmarked mint of a different and even cruder style. The last is rare in British hoards but is more often found in northern France, where Carausius had a continental foothold at the beginning of his usurpation. The important hoard from Rouen (originally about 400 coins found during road works in 1847) provides a possible mint location. Blackmoor continues into the reign of Allectus, by which time only the 'ML' and 'C' mints remained.

'Legitimist' hoards

Their overall lack of presence in Britain (in hoard and site finds) suggests there was some sort of difficulty with (or official indifference to) the supply of the reformed radiates to Britain (as opposed to the old debased Gallienus and Claudius II coins, which rapidly flooded in during the early 270s). Alternatively, they were perhaps unpopular in Britain through being tariffed at a higher value than the familiar pre-reformed radiates, and therefore not as useful. However, there are rare British examples of hoards containing virtually only the improved radiates of Aurelian and his successors, dubbed 'legitimist'. They consequently avoid the (pre-reformed) coins of the Gallic usurpers but, significantly, they also avoid the British usurpers, whose later coins bear the XXI mark (indicating an alloy of twenty parts bronze to one part silver) of the Aurelianic standard. Interestingly, during a brief period when Carausius attempted a *rapprochement* with the legitimate emperors, coins were also minted in the names of Diocletian and Maximian. There are only four such issues in the Blackmoor hoard, but legitimist hoards show a preference for these coins over those minted with the image of Carausius and Allectus (figure 27.3,4).

The best legitimist example is the Gloucester hoard of 15,544 radiates (figure 26). The hoard showed a remarkably selective range of issues: all but 0.4 per cent were Aurelianic-reformed coins; only 0.2 per cent carried the portraits of Carausius or Allectus; and a stray Victorinus

26. Found during city-centre building work in 1960 (within the remains of a Roman colonnaded building, perhaps a market hall), the Gloucester hoard comprised 15,544 radiates to 296, the eve of the re-absorption of rebel Britain, and was originally contained in a local Severn Valley coarse-ware jar and bowl (the latter providing a makeshift lid).

provided the solitary example of a Gallic emperor. Strikingly, despite its great size, its features were virtually unique in Britain until the 1998 discovery of the hoard of 3778 coins from Rogiet, Monmouthshire, and the 2000 discovery of an unusually mixed hoard of 434 reformed radiates alongside 206 pre-reformed radiates and 397 *nummi* of Diocletian's tetrarchy at Langtoft (hoard A), East Yorkshire. Coins of defeated Gallic and British usurpers may have been officially undesirable, but an alternative hypothesis to total demonetisation is to see Langtoft (so far unique in Britain but paralleled on the near continent) as an exceptional mixed hoard against a general habit that kept pre- and post-reformed radiates (and also *nummi* when they appear) separate. Indeed, with the paucity of reformed radiates in Britain, and with the strong element of negotiation needed in the ancient market-place and at the money-changer's table, the old debased radiates could have circulated at a lower value to the reformed radiates; effectively a different denomination with or without official sanction. Any tendency to segregate denominations would be perfectly in keeping with the hoarding habits of the first to the early third century.

27. A selection from the Gloucester hoard. 'Legitimist' radiates: (1) Aurelian, Rome (Sol), RIC 64 (275). (2) Probus, Ticinum (Fides), RIC 366 (276–82). (3) Diocletian, London, RIC 9 (292). (4) Maximian, London, RIC 34 (292). 3 and 4 were minted under the separatist regime in Britain. They were issued for only a short period during an attempt at *rapprochement* with the legitimate emperors. Despite this, they have a stronger presence than coins of Carausius and Allectus in hoards of this type: (5) Carausius, 'unmarked mint', RIC 878 (287–90). (6) Carausius, London, RIC 98var. (292). (7) Allectus, 'C' mint, RIC 91 (293–4). Numbers 3–7 all bear the Pax (peace) reverse type, common for Carausius and Allectus.

Radiate copies

Normanby and Blackmoor show that both the unreformed and the rarer reformed radiates circulated at least up to the end of British independence in 296. It is apparent that after their production terminated in 274, the diminishing pool of pre-reformed radiates was replenished with locally produced copies, often called 'barbarous' radiates (figure 25). The presence of copies in the circulation can be seen to increase over time, as attrition reduced the quantity of older official coins. A later radiate hoard usually contains a higher proportion of issues of Tetricus, 270–4, to those of his predecessor Victorinus, 268–70 (the newer coin spreading into the population as the older coin falls out), and an increased number of copies. This could be supply responding to demand, or part of a process exploiting silvered bronze (that also applied to the *nummus*, see below), in effect making the increasing radiate copies responsible for diminishing the number of official radiates.

After 274, the only new radiates produced were the reformed issues of Aurelian and his successors, but their tiny presence in the British circulation shows that, in all but the largest radiate hoards deposited after the fall of the Gallic Empire, the mint-date of the latest coins may only accidentally be close to the deposition date. Indeed, in studies of radiate copies based on their declining weight it is proposed that the latest examples in the Chalgrove hoard from Oxfordshire (4145 radiates to 278/9, 16.6 per cent copies, in two pots) were not produced before 282.

Early silvered-bronze *nummi*

The deposition of the Blackmoor hoard lies close in time and location to the presumed scene of the downfall of Allectus in battle, somewhere between Silchester and the Solent in 296. The event brought to Britain the new coinage based on the silvered-bronze *nummus*. It was just as base as its predecessor, but visually more impressive, no doubt intended (as had Aurelian's reform) to inspire fiscal confidence with size and careful manufacture. Quality control was aided by combinations of mint-markings, often identifying both mint and workshop, on a more formalised basis than had been done over the previous half-century, when mints across the empire began joining the city of Rome in minting imperial-style coinage. The London mint opened by Carausius joined this system for a brief but productive period until 326. A typical early *nummus* hoard, such as 'Prestwood B' from Buckinghamshire, shows that the local London issues are the most numerous, except only for those from Trier, the main centre of coin production for the north-western empire throughout the first half of the fourth century (figure 28). There is also a mix of coins of the other western mints, such as Lyons. At its introduction, the *nummus* was an impressive coin of around 10 grams, near the size of a first-century *as* but with a surface of silver (rarely surviving burial). This form did not long outlast the rule of Diocletian, and in a series of steps it was reduced to around the size of the old debased radiate, just over 3 grams, by 318 (lasting until the 330s when it sank below 2 grams). The repetitive reverse designs illustrated by Prestwood B are those depicting the Genius (spirit) of the Roman people, which give way to the sun-god Sol (on mints controlled by Constantine) around 310. It is interesting that the sun-god should be

28. A selection of coins from Prestwood B, which was metal-detected in 1999 and contains (alongside one radiate of 292/3) 734 *nummi* to 317, charting the rapid shrinkage of the *nummus* in the years following Diocletian's retirement in 305. (1) Constantius I, London (Genius), RIC VI 30var. (303–5). (2) Maximian, Rome (Moneta), RIC VI 105b (302–3). (3) Constantius I, Trier (Genius), RIC VI 655a (305–6). (4) Maximian, Lyons (Genius), RIC VI 288 (308). (5) Constantine I, Lyons (emperor and standards), RIC VI 299 (308–9). (6) Constantine I, Trier (Mars), RIC VI 829 (309). (7) Constantine I, Trier (Sol), RIC VI 865 (310–3). (8) Licinius I, London (Sol), RIC VII 60 (316).

honoured on the *nummus* as late as 317, long after the conversion of 312 claimed by Constantine. Although it may have been a consciously Christian decision to discontinue this – the final overtly pagan reverse type on everyday coinage in the west – its persistence (together with other pagan types) in hoards later in the century shows that there was little aversion to using it at an everyday level among a still largely unconverted populace.

Since its discovery during gas-pipeline trenching in 1994, the largest early *nummus* hoard from Britain is from Bridgend, South Wales, consisting of a coarse-ware pot and 1424 coins spanning 294–310. However, there is a far larger body of *nummus* hoards running exactly up to 317 than those that stop short of that date. A large-scale dumping, due to demonetisation, could be argued from this evidence, a repeat of the radiate-hoard situation. However, there are rare examples known of mixed coins from both sides of the 317 divide. As with the radiate–*nummus* changeover, perhaps, the old and the new coins were kept

29. The Grassmoor hoard (1375 *nummi* to 340). Hoards of the middle Constantinian period mostly run through a succession of religiously ambiguous stock reverse types.

separate by hoarders, and the post-317 *nummus* caused some sort of *de facto* or *de jure* denominational relationship rather than a complete abandonment of the old coin. This would help to explain why so many hoards containing pre-317 coins run exactly up to that date: they would have had a much longer time to be assembled, long after all possible issues had entered the circulation.

Later base-silver *nummi*

The 317 change has little else in common with 274, since the coins produced in the 320s and 330s dwarf the preceding *nummus* period in both the hoard and archaeological site record – the reverse of the radiate situation. Hoarding activity of post-318 (and especially post-330) *nummi* reached a peak nearly equalling the old debased-radiate hoards (figures 29 and 30). The first coins of the new series introduced by Constantine (figure 30.1) borrowed a design from a (pure) silver coin issued five years earlier, and no doubt this choice helped to draw attention to the improved, but still tiny, silver content (briefly doubled from around 1.5 to 3 per cent).

***Fel Temp* reform and Magnentian hoards**

In 348 a suite of three denominations of *nummi* was introduced. All bore the legend *Fel(icium) Temp(orum) Reparatio* – 'happy times restored' – probably to commemorate the 1100th anniversary of Rome's foundation. Unlike in the last revision of the coinage in 317, *Fel Temp* coins were often hoarded indiscriminately with pre-348 issues. A good example is the Coleshill hoard from near Birmingham, consisting of 3237 coins uncovered along with fragments of their coarse-ware container during house building in 1931. Although *Fel Temp* issues made up a significant part of the hoard, just under 60 per cent were pre-348 *nummi*, mostly from the 330s and 340s. Britain was deep within the territory of Magnentius, and most of the post-350 *nummi* in Coleshill are of the usurper (or his brother and imperial partner, Decentius). There are no divergent trends at this period of hoards selecting legitimate emperors (probably because of the comprehensive nature of the demonetisations that followed Magnentius's death; see below).

The hoard found at Wokingham, Berkshire, in 1970 is different from hoards such as Coleshill in that virtually only the larger post-348 coins have been selected for hoarding. This remains the best example of such hoards, sometimes called 'Magnentian' (figure 31). The coinage of Magnentius has a more varied repertoire of reverse types than those produced by Constantius II in the east. Just before his downfall he even introduced a new bronze denomination, around the size of the old Diocletianic *nummus*, bearing the Christogram – the victory symbol of

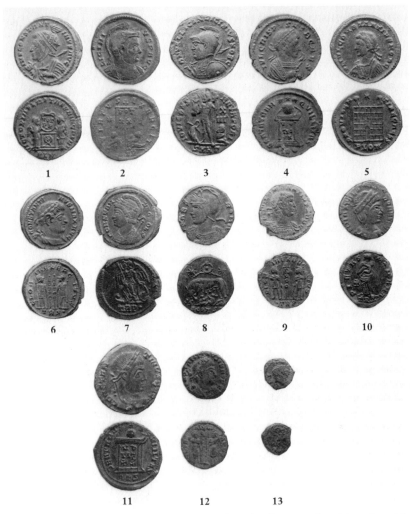

30. A selection of official and barbarous *nummi* from the Grassmoor hoard (together with number 13 from the Hockwold, Norfolk, hoard of *nummus* copies). (1) Constantine I, London (two Victories), RIC VII 168 (320). (2) Licinius I, Trier (captives under banner), RIC VII— (321). (3) Licinius II, Heraclea (Jupiter), RIC VII 54 (321–4). (4) Crispus, Trier (altar), RIC VII 379 (321). (5) Constantius II, London (fort gate), RIC VII 298 (324–5). (6) Constantine I, Trier (two soldiers and two standards), RIC VII 526 (330–5). (7) Constantinopolis, Trier (Victory), RIC VII 530 (330–1). (8) Roma, Arles (wolf suckling Romulus and Remus), RIC VII 373 (333). (9) Constantius II, Trier (two soldiers and a standard), RIC VII 592 (335–7). (10) Theodora, Trier (Pietas), RIC VIII 43 (337–40). *Nummus* copies: (11) 'Constantine I' (altar) (compare with 4); (12) 'Constantine II' (two soldiers and two standards) (compare with 6); (13) Constantinopolis (Victory) (compare with 7).

31. The Wokingham hoard was discovered by a complete fluke, spotted on the surface of a ploughed field by a passer-by walking her dogs. A clue to what was there was given by a potsherd with a coin-shaped corrosion ring. Subsequent archaeological investigation revealed the base of a decorated fourth-century Oxfordshire beaker and the remainder of the coins. (Pot drawing [1:4] by M. G. Fulford)

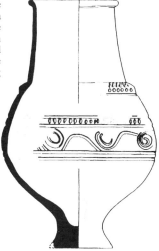

Constantine (ironically, his opponent's father). At this point, the Trier mint continued to be the principal supplier (42 per cent of the regular coins from Wokingham). However, a new mint was also opened for the duration of the usurpation at Amiens. Given their particularly high presence in the Romano-British coin circulation (one-third of the regular coins from Wokingham), it is possible that this mint, strategically placed on the Somme river for shipments to the south coast of Britain, was opened especially to supply the island. A more recent Magnentian hoard discovery was metal-detected in 1989 at Wheaton Aston in Staffordshire (figure 32). Although much smaller (484 *nummi*), it also scrupulously avoided the pre-348 issues but, interestingly, contained a few of Constantine I's pre-318 Sol *nummi* – presumably still acceptable because they were roughly the same size as the bigger *Fel Temp* coins. The underlying reasons for the two different compositional groups represented by Wokingham and Coleshill are difficult to understand. If different sizes of coins were being accepted as different denominations, then we have mixed (Coleshill-type) hoards forming the majority for this period – the opposite of the early empire, in which mixed hoards are the rarity.

Diademed *nummus* copies

An interesting change seen on late Roman coins is the adoption of the diadem (jewelled headband), replacing the traditional laurel wreath, on coinage from the late 320s. A symbol of Greek kingship, it effectively associated Constantine with Alexander, another monarch called 'the

32. A selection of the *nummi* from the Wheaton Aston hoard. (1) Constantius II (soldier spearing enemy horseman), Aquileia, RIC VIII 113 (348–50). (2) Magnentius, Amiens (two victories), RIC VIII 23 (350–3). (3) Decentius, Trier (Christogram), RIC VIII 324 (350–3). (4) Magnentius (rider spearing foe), irregular copy (350–3). (5) Constantius II, Trier (soldier spearing enemy horseman), RIC VIII 350 (353–4).

great'. The 330s–350s are characterised by another copying 'epidemic' akin to the earlier barbarous radiates (figure 30.11–13). Like the radiates, they are often of unconvincing style, and they were produced on a scale that suggests that the authorities might have been turning a blind eye to their production, or were unable to counter it. Again, they are prominent among coin finds in northern Gaul and Britain, suggesting that their production was a response to supply problems, probably aggravated by a *nummus* production gap during the early 340s and the demonetisation of some categories of base coins after 354. However, the picture is clearly a more complicated one, since hoards such as Coleshill, with 7.4 per cent imitations, show that issues were copied as soon as they appeared, as they follow quite closely the weights of the issues they imitate. In addition, the copies of the post-348 coins of Coleshill, and Magnentian hoards such as Wokingham (22.1 per cent irregular), show that coins of Magnentius, although quickly demonetised, were also copiously copied. Unlike the Claudian bronze copying epidemic, base-silver (*nummi* and radiates) copies must have been a response to a number of factors relating to changes in the coinage, both physical (size and silver content) and presumably others, such as laws and market forces. They were likely to have been the by-products from the melting down of regular issues to recover the silver (a practice specifically legislated against in 348), the remaining base material (which contained residual amounts of the unrecovered silver) being recycled as copies.

Magnentian hoards such as Wokingham and mixed hoards such as Coleshill end *c*.353–4, around the time of the downfall of the usurper. It is imagined that Magnentius's coins were outlawed by the vengeful Constantius II: they survive only in tiny numbers from later hoards. If so, it came as part of the package of demonetisations of 354, which were probably more concerned with the massive exploitation of debased-silver coins by forgers. For the first time in Roman imperial monetary history, we can be certain that a large-scale demonetisation occurred since the law itself survives. Among the condemned coins were the larger silvered bronzes, vaguely referred to as *pecuniae maiorinae*, 'big coins'. Also outlawed was a coin called the *centenionalis* (a 'one-hundredth' in the same sense as a modern penny or cent), presumably the pre-348 *nummi*. What *was* allowed? From this point onwards, only the third and smallest module *Fel Temp* coin remained in production (the legend soon dropped in favour of new slogans and designs in 358). Weighing around 2.5 grams, unlike the others it was apparently intended to be plain unadorned bronze and had been largely omitted from the Magnentian system. As far as Roman Britain was concerned, the erratic experiment with silvered bronze was over: the empire had returned to producing a tri-metallic coinage of gold, silver and bronze.

5
Hoards of the later fourth and fifth centuries: the end of Roman Britain and beyond

Britain continued to be a valuable asset to the later fourth-century empire. Although its cities were decaying, its agriculture still fed the army – especially with shipments to the all-important Rhine frontier. Despite reports of massed barbarian incursions during the 360s, the end for Roman Britain did not come until the ineffectual rule of Honorius (393–423). Regular supplies of new bronze and silver coins dried up by 402, no doubt fuelling army discontent with the disruption on the Continent. The Roman army in Britain threw up a succession of usurpers ending with Constantine III (407–11), who drew off the island's mobile field army and crossed the Channel to rectify the situation, never to return (figure 33). Just before their departure, the latest supplies of gold coin ceased by 406 and, subsequently, only a few coins of the usurper came to Britain after his establishment in Gaul. With no field army, the civilian British population had to look to their own defence, presumably involving prominent public citizens coming to the fore to organise mercenary forces when barbarian attacks next arose, as they did around 409–10.

The return of silver and gold
   The most striking aspect of the coinage of the final phase of Roman Britain was the reappearance of gold and good silver (the latter now divorced from its unsuccessful alloying with bronze). This might in part be explained by the increased availability of precious metals from the looting of the pagan temples by the first Christian emperors. It is also due to a new approach to monetary exchange that helped to stabilise the 'serious' precious-metal coinage at the expense of the small change, ending the reform–debasement–inflation cycles of the mid third to the mid fourth century, and setting the character of the coinage that would last well into Byzantine times.
   The runaway price inflation was tackled in two ways. First, money was often bypassed altogether, as soldiers and officials received much of their wages as payment in kind. A soldier might receive a five-yearly bonus of five gold *solidi* but was fed and equipped through direct requisitions to a yearly equivalent to four *solidi*. Second, wealth had found a safe haven in the gold and silver coins, which maintained their spending power by effectively floating in value against the bronze

33. Richborough in Kent, the last known base of the Second Legion. The latest issues of Roman bronze coins have a strong presence at this 'Saxon Shore' fort, and no fewer than ten bronze hoards ending 402 were excavated. There would have been scant opportunity for soldiers to recover them if they had joined Constantine III's expedition. The bronze *nummus* was the loser in the late Roman coinage system, shrinking over the last four decades of the fourth century from 18 mm to 11 mm in diameter (from just under 3 grams to less than 1.5 grams). The appearance of the coins is miserable (inset is a late fourth-century *nummus* from the Hoxne hoard, RIC X cf. 1247, 395–402), and preservation is not helped by their poor leaded-bronze alloy, and relatively few final-period bronze hoards from Britain have been closely studied or kept together. Typical features show that the output of the mint of Trier for bronze diminished while the mint of Arles dominated until the general cessation of bronze minting in the west outside Rome *c*.395. Hoards of bronzes from this time could also contain a mishmash of low-denomination issues stretching back to the third century. These coins were now such insignificant tokens that any small base coin could be put to good use. (Richborough photograph courtesy of P. Clayton)

nummus, which still represented an uncertain multiple of notional *denarii*. The cost of gold could then rise apace with other goods: in 324 it cost 313,200 *denarii* per (Roman) pound; by the middle of the fourth century, 331,200,000 *denarii* and rising. A side effect was that the difference between precious-metal coin and other forms of bullion became blurred. At the time of imperial 'coronations', a Roman soldier's bonus would include an additional pound ingot of silver. Ingots could carry similar mint-marks to coins (figure 34). This close relationship between coin and ingot is also demonstrated in the official process of melting down

34. Silver ingot from the Canterbury hoard (of late Roman bullion, coins, jewellery and precious tableware), found during 1960s road building. OF LEO / TR•PS / P•I * identifies it as: from Leo's workshop (*OFficina*) / Trier mint • refined silver / one pound (at fourth-century weight value = 4 *solidi*). The formula TRPS, *TReveri PuSulatum*, is the same as appears on silver coins from the mint of Trier in the late fourth century. While more than forty late-Roman silver ingots have been found on the Continent, over twenty have been found in the British Isles alone – a disproportionate number for an area containing 10 per cent of the Roman army. (Actual length *c.*14 cm; weight 321.5 grams.)

gold and silver coins collected as tax in order to ship them back in ingot form to be restruck.

The Hoxne treasure

The exceptionally rich Hoxne (Suffolk) find (figure 35) is very informative about coin use at the end of Roman Britain. It was discovered by chance in 1992 during a search with a metal detector for a lost hammer, and prompt reporting allowed archaeologists to uncover the find in detail. (In stark contrast, the richest-ever British find of Roman gold coins, found nearby at Eye in 1781, 600 *solidi* in a lead box, was long ago dispersed. They were of the same period as Hoxne, and supposedly found 4 miles [6 km] away, but records are so vague that it cannot be ruled out that Eye and Hoxne were part of one huge deposit.) Hoxne consists of just over 15,000 coins (24 bronze, the rest gold and silver), alongside around 200 gold and silver objects: jewellery, fine tableware and toilet instruments. The precious objects of Hoxne were not just ornaments, they were as much a store of wealth as the coins.

Hoxne shows the return to a coinage system based on high-quality silver. The main silver unit, the so-called *siliqua*, was produced from early in the fourth century but did not become an important part of the circulation until 358, when it was reduced in weight to about 2 grams (figure 36). Alongside Hoxne's *siliquae* were sixty 4.5 gram silver multiples, called *miliarenses* (figure 37). These impressive coins are rare and are usually found only in relatively small numbers alongside significant *siliquae* hoards. Gold, too, made a comeback in the circulation of the later fourth century. Hoxne contained 580 gold *solidi*, a lighter (around 4.5 grams) version of the earlier *aureus* (figure 38). Interestingly, the total weight value of all the silver coins (at the fifth-century standard of five *solidi* to a pound of silver) from Hoxne comes only to the equivalent of 494 *solidi*, making a hypothetical total of 1074 *solidi* worth of coins. The Hoxne treasure stands high in comparison even to the annual salaries of less humble occupations than soldiering, which are occasionally mentioned in late Roman writings: public doctor –

35. The Hoxne hoard. Micro-excavation revealed the care with which the coins and ornamental utensils had been secreted in a wooden chest (60 x 45 x 30 cm), which survived only as a colour change in the soil alongside some rusted iron fittings. Some of the objects name seven previous owners, although whether they were members of one family, the Aurelii (the family name of one individual, a man called Ursicinus), is impossible to say. However, they were clearly wealthy and of high status, one inscription referring to a *domina* (lady or mistress), Juliana.

36. A selection of Hoxne's 14,137 *siliquae*. (1) Constantius II, Arles (record of imperial vows in wreath), RIC VIII 261/291 (355–60). (2) Julian, Arles (vows), RIC VIII 309 (362–3). (3) Valentinian I, Constantinople (vows), RIC IX 36a (367–75). (4) Valens, Arles (emperor with Christogram banner), RIC IX 6c (364–7). (5) Valentinian II, Trier (Victory), RIC IX 43 (375–9). (6) Theodosius I, Trier (Constantinopolis), RIC IX 55a (378–88). (7) Flavius Victor, Aquileia (facing Roma enthroned), RIC IX 54b (387–8). (8) Honorius, Milan (Roma sitting on cuirass), RIC X 1228b (395–402). (9) Honorius, Rome (Roma), RIC X 1267 (404–8). (10) Constantine III, Lyons (Roma), RIC X 1529 (407–8). 11–13 are clipped *siliquae* showing that silver was repeatedly removed from the edges until, in the worst examples, only the bust of the emperor was left. (11) Gratian, Trier (*Urbs Roma*), RIC IX 27f/45c (367–78). 12 and 13 are same type and mint (but emperor uncertain), 14 and 15 are copies made of good silver, but with slightly scrambled designs and mint marks, of Theodosius I (14) and Arcadius (15).

1   2   3   4

1   2   3

4   5   6

37. (Above) A selection of silver *miliarenses* from Hoxne. Britain, being unusually rich in silver hoards of this period, is a good source for these impressive coins. (1) Valens, Rome (Victory inscribing vows), RIC IX 8b (364–7). (2) Gratian, Trier (vows), RIC IX 23d (367–75). (3) Magnus Maximus, Trier (emperor and banner), RIC IX 82 (383–8). (4) Eugenius, Trier (emperor and banner), RIC IX 104 (392–5).

38. (Left) A selection of gold *solidi* from Hoxne. (1) Valentinian I, Trier (two emperors), RIC IX 17b (367–75). (2) Gratian, Trier (two emperors), RIC IX 39d (375–8). (3) Theodosius I, Constantinople (Constantinopolis), RIC IX 44c (379–83). (4) Valentinian II, Trier (two emperors), RIC IX 90a (388–92). (5) Arcadius, Milan (emperor spurning foe), RIC X 1205c (395–402). (6) Honorius, Ravenna (emperor spurning foe), RIC X 1286a (402–6).

sixty *solidi*; rhetoric professor – seventy-two *solidi*; legal assessor – fifty-six *solidi*.

Britain is not exceptional for gold hoards of this period compared to the rest of the empire. Where the island excels over the rest of the empire is with hoards of late Roman silver (occasionally mixed with gold or bronze). Of all known Roman hoards of silver coins closing 388–410, 80 per cent are from Britain. Furthermore, there appears to be a habit of silver hoarding in certain areas of late Roman Britain. The empire-wide pattern is easier to answer, in that the concentration within Britain (which the graph on page 9 also shows as a chronological concentration) is explained by the fact that no fresh coin entered Britain after the scarce issues of Constantine III. This means that only old coins continued to be used during the fifth century in Britain (one of the many problems with archaeological dating in this 'dark' century), giving an exaggerated impression of a concentration of one period when the evidence really represents several over the course of the earlier part of the fifth century. While silver coin use continued in Britain, the Continent (with the exception of Romania, another area locked outside the empire) was showing a move to reliance on gold coins.

Hoards closing in the first decade of the fifth century (from the 'end' of Roman Britain) can be ranked in order of the diminishing ratios of the coins of 364–78 (the house of Valentinian I) against the newer coins of 395–402 (the joint rule of Honorius with his brother Arcadius). This suggests a pattern formed over a period of time, as implied by cycles of hoards from earlier periods that are not cut off and have progressively later closing dates. Recycled coinage therefore continued to be used over a considerable period of time after 410.

The ordering of fifth-century hoards highlights the increasing presence over time of two other phenomena – forgeries made of good-quality silver, and progressive stages of clipping (figure 36.11–15). The latter activity occurred only in Britain, and, together with the appearance of copies (whose source of silver seems to have come from official coins), must be connected with the closing of the Romano-British silver coin pool after 402. Clipping was so obvious and widespread that, if not initiated by the post-Romano-British authorities, they had become powerless to stop it. Although some of the recovered silver went to make copies, much more must have gone elsewhere (figure 39). (Seventeenth-century English Civil War hoards show that clipping flourished in times of anarchy and upheaval: it was unofficially tolerated for the sake of everyday convenience with silver coins but not with gold – an interesting parallel to the observable results from the fifth century.)

Stanchester (cover illustration) is an earlier type of fifth-century silver hoard. Its typical features are relatively unclipped *siliquae*, few forgeries, and a strong presence of *miliarenses*. But is this due to the selectivity of the hoarder or an as yet untouched coinage? In contrast to Stanchester, Hoxne shows characteristic features of the latest Romano-British coin hoards: it contained quantities of precious ornaments, while its *siliquae*, most severely clipped, are dominated by issues of 395–402 – the latest to be regularly supplied to Britain. How long it took for Hoxne's final coin of 408 to find its way to Britain and be buried is guesswork. With the absence of more recent Roman coins in British hoards, such unempirical hoard-composition evidence is the only way to chart the persistence of coin use. They suggest a system in its death throes: while anarchic clipping sapped confidence in the face value of the silver coinage, the intrinsically valuable ornaments or scrap that increasingly

39. The Coleraine hoard from Northern Ireland, hidden far from Roman Britain, and discovered by ditch diggers in 1854. It contains Roman silver tableware and ingots, alongside 1506 coins up to 408. Much of the material has been chopped up into easily measurable and shareable amounts of loot: the result of raiding or extortion or diplomatic payments. Alongside officially stamped 'double-axe' ingots, similar to figure 34, are other unmarked ingots of cruder form (some reminiscent of the jeweller's ingots in figure 13). Perhaps some of the silver clipped from the edges of coins seen in hoards like Hoxne found their way into this format.

accompanied them heralded the fate of coined gold and silver.

Could the concentration of such silver hoards in Britain (nearly one hundred known so far) also be the result of barbarian incursions, treasure left unclaimed by wealthy Britons from areas that had been 'ethnically cleansed' of their elite? Perhaps an increasingly rapacious local authority, desperate to pay for mercenary protection, had driven men (among them perhaps Aurelius Urscinius of Hoxne) to secrete their liquefiable assets because they could not bear to see their wealth squandered to buy time for a failing regime. They would then vainly have hoped for some future accommodation when they could return to their economic position in the community. Fifth-century Romano-British hoards cluster in south-central England (Hampshire, Wiltshire, Somerset, etc) and the area comprising East Anglia and Lincolnshire, whereas site finds do not show such restriction. Could these reflect areas where the Anglo-Saxons were least accommodating (or the Romano-British most stubbornly resistant)? Unfortunately, there is no easy answer and the prevalence of silver hoards and of the clipping of coins remains an enigmatic and very British phenomenon, the reasons behind which await further knowledge of how Roman Britain became Anglo-Saxon England.

Epilogue: the Patching hoard

Until 1997, all lists of Roman hoards in Britain would end with a tiny group containing the rare coins of Constantine III. These include the aforementioned Hoxne and Eye hoards as well as Stanmore (Middlesex, 1781), to which could be added hoards of scrapped silver bullion from beyond the empire at Coleraine, Northern Ireland (figure 39), and Traprain Law, East Lothian, since the material must have come from Roman Britain. However, the discovery of the Patching hoard from West Sussex was unprecedented because twenty-one out of fifty coins post-dated the reign of Constantine III and closed about 465 (figure 40). The hoard contents must have been gathered by the hoarder from both Britain (some *siliquae* were clipped and must have been from a British source) and the Continent. Late fifth-century Gaul consisted of some remnants of the old Roman authorities as well as barbarian kingdoms that had managed to assimilate (or be assimilated by, depending on one's point of view) the late Roman societies they had conquered. Unlike in Anglo-Saxon England, these warrior peoples were still able to take advantage of civil society and its administrative structures, and coinage continued to be produced (usually recognising the technical overlordship of some distant and impotent Roman emperor). Gold had now become favoured over silver coinage in the fifth century, especially for the Germanic peoples, who used it for large-scale transactions such as compensation payments or gift exchange and seemingly little else.

40. Patching (selection illustrated) was detected as a scattered hoard (disturbed by ploughing) and consisted of twenty-three gold *solidi*, three silver *miliarenses* and twenty-three silver *siliquae*, along with two gold rings and a Roman pound of scrapped silver bullion. The latest coin is a *solidus* in the name of Libius Severus (461–5).

Most of the mid-fifth-century coins in Patching are gold *solidi* of Honorius (whose reign extended to 423), his successor Valentinian III (425–55), and Theodosius II (eastern emperor 402–50). Also present are eight *solidi* (and three silver *siliquae*) of the Visigoths, who dominated much of Gaul at the time. There were also three Visigothic silver *siliquae* in Patching, which, like the *solidi*, are distinguished from the Roman coins they copy by their crudely imitative style. Roman and Visigothic coins are known from later-fifth-century British contexts, although only as occasional solitary examples, often from Anglo-Saxon cemetery sites. Sometimes they are pierced or mounted as jewellery (figure 41), but never before had they been found as a part of a coin hoard. Perhaps these imported coins represent part of the same links established when later-fifth-century continental pottery began to make a reappearance in Britain (albeit in areas far to the west of Patching such as South Cadbury

41. Two Anglo-Saxon coin pendants from Oxborough, Norfolk. (Far left) Although reused as fifth-century jewellery, the coin is a silver *denarius* of Severus Alexander (222–35). (Near left) A Visigothic *solidus* in the name of Libius Severus (461–5).

42. Roman coins lingered on as everyday objects in Anglo-Saxon times. This balance and weights set was excavated at Dover from a pagan warrior's grave of the sixth century. It was used to weigh out pieces of bullion, but the weights were fourteen worn and battered Roman base-metal coins from the first to the fourth century, scratched with weight markings. No longer money, the 'hoard' embodies the transition from Roman Britain to Anglo-Saxon England.

in Somerset). Because Patching contains this unique mix, the continental coins provide a *terminus post quem* that shows that the remnants of recycled coins that had arrived prior to the isolation of Britain could potentially continue in service for most of the fifth century. However, the very singularity of Patching would suggest that coin use beyond the middle of the fifth century was a shadow of that during the initial decades, confirming rather than contradicting the assumed disruption of the 440s (the presumed latest possible *deposition* date of hoards such as Hoxne), when Romano-Britons were reported appealing for help in the face of massed barbarian attack around the year 446.

The Patching coins were buried within sight of Highdown Hill. A reused prehistoric hillfort, and Sussex's most important early Saxon site, Highdown also has contemporary evidence of a late Roman (or 'sub-Roman') presence. This has led archaeologists to propose a picture of Saxon mercenaries led by a local British magnate paymaster. (Interestingly, the Stanchester coin hoard takes its name from a nearby late-Roman villa site. The excavators have, by virtue of its Saxon name, whose ending is more usually applied to walled settlements, proposed that it could have remained an influential centre beyond the end of Roman Britain. The contexts of Stanchester and Patching, deposited at either ends of the fifth century, seem very different and perhaps it was a sign of the times that surviving British authority had to seek safer refuge.) Perhaps Patching represents payments either already received by mercenaries or intended to be made by 'sub-Roman' Britons, only to be left unclaimed when the founders of Sussex decided to take control, rather than payment, around the 470s.

6
Museums

This chapter lists the coin hoards cited in this book and indicates, where applicable, the United Kingdom museum collection where each is now held. Full details of these museums and of some others with coin galleries will be found at the end of the chapter. Readers should bear in mind that the material may not always be on public display and are advised to check the dates and times of opening before making a visit. The hoards are numbered and the numbers are used to indicate the locations of the findspots on the map on page 69.

Early hoards
1. Alton, Hampshire (gold): The British Museum.
2. Bredgar, Kent (gold): The British Museum.
3. Eriswell, Norfolk (silver): The British Museum.
4. Howe, Norfolk (gold and silver): The British Museum.
5. Kempsford, Gloucestershire (bronze).
6. North Suffolk forger's hoard (plated silver): The British Museum.
7. Owslebury, Hampshire (silver).
8. Shillington, Bedfordshire (gold): Luton Museum.
9. Timsbury, Hampshire (bronze).

Hoards from the time of the developed province
10. Birdoswald, Cumbria (silver): Tullie House Museum.
11. Corbridge, Northumberland (gold): The British Museum.
12. Curridge, Berkshire (bronze): West Berkshire Museum.
13. Didcot, Oxfordshire (gold): The British Museum.
14. Edston, Scottish Borders (silver): National Museums of Scotland.
15. Falkirk (silver): National Museums of Scotland.

43. The Shapwick Villa treasure on display in Somerset County Museum, Taunton. (Photograph: R. A. Abdy)

16. Gare, Cornwall (bronze): Royal Cornwall Museum.
17. Lawrence Weston, Bristol: The British Museum (small sample).
18. M1, Leicestershire (silver).
19. Mattishall, Norfolk (silver): Norwich Castle Museum.
20. Plantation Place, City of London (gold): Museum of London.
21. Shapwick Villa, Somerset (gold): Somerset County Museum.
22. Snettisham (jeweller's hoard), Norfolk (silver and bronze): British Museum.

Late Roman silvered-bronze hoards: radiates
23. Blackmoor, Hampshire: The British Museum and Fitzwilliam Museum (samples only).
24. Chalgrove, Oxfordshire.
25. Cunetio, Wiltshire: The British Museum and Wiltshire Heritage Museum.
26. Gloucester: Gloucester City Museum and The British Museum.
27. Normanby, Lincolnshire: The British Museum (sample); Lincoln City and County Museum (pot).
28. Tinwell, Rutland: Rutland County Museum.

Late Roman silvered-bronze hoards: *nummi*
29. Bridgend, South Wales: National Museum of Wales.
30. Coleshill, Warwickshire: Birmingham Museum.
31. Grassmoor, Derbyshire: samples in Chesterfield Museum and The British Museum.
32. Hockwold, Norfolk: The British Museum.
33. Langtoft, East Yorkshire.
34. Prestwood B, Buckinghamshire: Buckinghamshire County Museum.
35. Wheaton Aston, Staffordshire.
36. Wokingham, Berkshire: Museum of Reading.

Hoards from the end of Roman Britain and beyond
37. Canterbury, Kent: Canterbury Roman Museum.
38. Coleraine, Northern Ireland: The British Museum.
39. Dover Anglo-Saxon Cemetery, Kent (balance and coin-weights): The British Museum.
40. Hoxne, Suffolk: The British Museum.
41. Patching, West Sussex: Worthing Museum.
42. Richborough, Kent: Richborough Site Museum.
43. Stanchester, Wiltshire: Wiltshire Heritage Museum.
44. Traprain Law, East Lothian: National Museums of Scotland.

Museums
Birmingham Museum, Chamberlain Square, Birmingham B3 3DH. Telephone: 0121 303 2834. Website: www.birmingham.gov.uk/bmag
The British Museum, Great Russell Street, London WC1B 3DG. Telephone: 020 7323 8000. Website: www.thebritishmuseum.ac.uk
Buckinghamshire County Museum, Church Street, Aylesbury, Buckinghamshire HP20 2QP. Telephone: 01296 331441.
Canterbury Roman Museum, Longmarket, Butchery Lane, Canterbury, Kent CT1 2RA. Telephone: 01227 785575. Website: www.canterbury-museum.co.uk
Castle Museum, Colchester Castle, Castle Park, Colchester, Essex CO1 1TJ. Telephone: 01206 282932. Website: www.colchestermuseums.org.uk

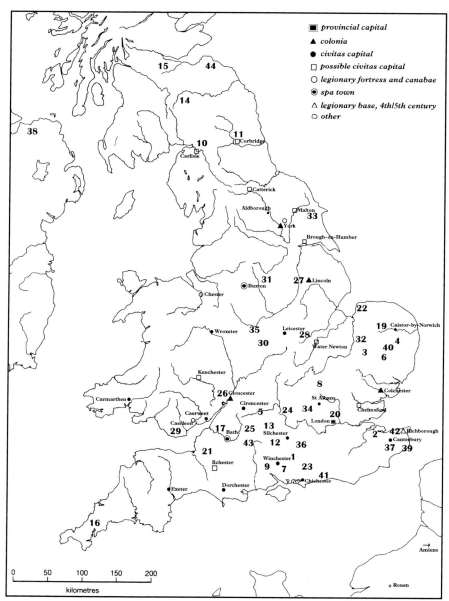

44. Map showing the findspots of the hoards described in this book. The numbers refer to the list of hoards on pages 67–8.

Chesterfield Museum and Art Gallery, St Mary's Gate, Chesterfield, Derbyshire S41 7TY. Telephone: 01246 245727.

Fitzwilliam Museum, Trumpington Street, Cambridge CB2 1RB. Telephone: 01223 332900. Website: www.fitzmuseum.cam.ac.uk

Gloucester City Museum and Art Gallery, Brunswick Road, Gloucester GL1 1HP. Telephone: 01452 524131. Website: www.mylife.gloucester.gov.uk

Hunterian Museum, The University of Glasgow, Glasgow G12 8QQ. Telephone: 0141 330 4221. Website: www.hunterian.gla.ac.uk

Lincoln City and County Museum, 12 Friars Lane, Lincoln LN2 5AL. Telephone: 01522 530401.

Luton Museum, Wardown Park, Luton, Bedfordshire LU2 7HA. Telephone: 01582 746722. Website: www.luton.gov.uk

Manchester Museum, The University of Manchester, Oxford Road, Manchester M13 9PL. Telephone: 0161 275 2634. Website: www.museum.man.ac.uk

Museum of London, 150 London Wall, London EC2Y 5HN. Telephone: 020 7600 3699. Website: www.museumoflondon.org.uk

Museum of Reading, Blagrave Street, Reading, Berkshire RG1 1QH. Telephone: 0118 939 9800. Website: www.readingmuseum.org

National Museum of Wales, Cathays Park, Cardiff CF10 3NP. Telephone: 029 2039 7951. Website: www.nmgw.ac.uk

National Museums of Scotland, Chambers Street, Edinburgh EH1 1JF. Telephone: 0131 225 7534. Website: www.nms.ac.uk

Norwich Castle Museum, Castle Meadow, Norwich NR1 3JU. Telephone: 01603 493625. Website: www.norfolk.gov.uk/tourism/museums/castle.htm

Richborough Castle Museum, Richborough Castle, Richborough, Sandwich, Kent CT13 9JW. Telephone: 01304 612013. Website: www.english-heritage.org.uk

Royal Cornwall Museum, River Street, Truro, Cornwall TR12 2SJ. Telephone: 01872 272205. Website: www.royalcornwallmuseum.org.uk

Rutland County Museum, Catmos Street, Oakham, Rutland LE15 6HW. Telephone: 01572 758440. Website: www.rutnet.co.uk

Somerset County Museum, Taunton Castle, Castle Green, Taunton, Somerset TA1 4AA. Telephone: 01823 320200. Website: www.somerset.gov.uk/museums

Tullie House Museum, Castle Street, Carlisle, Cumbria CA3 8TP. Telephone: 01228 534781. Website: www.tulliehouse.co.uk

West Berkshire Museum, The Wharf, Newbury, Berkshire RG14 5AS. Telephone: 01635 30511. Website: www.westberks.gov.uk

Wiltshire Heritage Museum, 41 Long Street, Devizes, Wiltshire SN10 1NS. Telephone: 01380 727369. Website: www.wiltshireheritage.org.uk

Worthing Museum, Chapel Road, Worthing, West Sussex BN11 1HP. Telephone: 01903 239999. Website: www.worthing.gov.uk

Other useful contacts

For recording and reporting of finds of ancient coins see www.finds.org.uk For details of museums in the United Kingdom see www.24hourmuseum.org.uk

7
Further reading

Roman Britain

Faulkner, N. *The Decline and Fall of Roman Britain*. Tempus, 2001. Despite its title, it covers the whole period of Roman Britain; a very readable and up-to-date archaeological and historical narrative.

Jones, B., and Mattingly, D. *An Atlas of Roman Britain*. Blackwell, 1990; reprinted, Oxbow, 2002.

Potter, T.W. *Roman Britain*. British Museum Press, 1997.

Potter, T.W., and Johns, C. *Roman Britain*. British Museum Press, 1992.

Roman Empire

Reece, R. *The Later Roman Empire: An Archaeology AD 150–600*. Tempus, 1999.

Wells, C. *The Roman Empire*. Fontana, 1992. For the early empire.

General introduction to coins

Besly, E. *Loose Change: A Guide to Common Coins and Medals*. National Museums of Wales, 1997.

Burnett, A. *Coins*. British Museum Press, 1991.

Casey, P.J. *Understanding Ancient Coins*. Batsford, 1986.

Williams, J. (editor). *Money – A History*. British Museum Press, 1997.

Introduction to Roman coins

Burnett, A. *Coinage in the Roman World*. Seaby, 1987.

Casey, P.J. *Roman Coinage in Britain*. Shire, 1980; third edition, reprinted 2002.

Reece, R. *Coinage in Roman Britain*. Seaby, 1987.

Specific Roman coin hoards/assemblages

Besly, E., and Bland, R. *The Cunetio Treasure: Roman Coinage from the Third Century AD*. British Museum Press, 1983.

Bland, R., and Johns, C. *The Hoxne Treasure: An Illustrated Introduction*. British Museum Press, 1993.

Guest, P. *The Late Roman Gold and Silver Coins from the Hoxne Treasure*. British Museum Press, forthcoming.

Johns, C. (editor). *The Snettisham Roman Jeweller's Hoard*. British Museum Press, 1997.

Minnitt, S. *The Shapwick Treasure*. Taunton, 2001.

Robertson A.S. 'Romano-British Coin Hoards: Their Numismatic, Archaeological and Historical Significance' in *Coins and the Archaeologist*, edited by Casey and Reece, Seaby, 1988.

Various editors. *Coin Hoards from Roman Britain*. Volumes 1–10, British Museum Press; volume 11, Royal Numismatic Society. Note that volumes 1–9 are summarised in: Robertson, A.S. *An Inventory of Romano-British Coin Hoards*. Edited by R. Hobbs and T.V. Buttrey. Royal Numismatic Society, 2000.

Walker, D.R. 'The Roman Coins' in Cunliffe, B. *The Finds from the Sacred Spring* (volume 2 of *The Temple of Sulis Minerva at Bath*). Oxford, 1988, 281–339.

72

Index

Page numbers in italic refer to illustrations